# POETRY'S NATURE

CLARENDON LECTURES IN ENGLISH SERIES

Justin Bradshaw, "Waterfall Near Corchiano," 2023. Private collection.

SUSAN STEWART

# POETRY'S NATURE

*Four Lectures*

Great Clarendon Street, Oxford, OX2 6DP,
United Kingdom

Oxford University Press is a department of the University of Oxford.
It furthers the University's objective of excellence in research, scholarship,
and education by publishing worldwide. Oxford is a registered trade mark of
Oxford University Press in the UK and in certain other countries

© Susan Stewart 2025

The moral rights of the author have been asserted.

All rights reserved. No part of this publication may be reproduced, stored in a retrieval system, transmitted, used for text and data mining, or used for training artificial intelligence, in any form or by any means, without the prior permission in writing of Oxford University Press, or as expressly permitted by law, by licence or under terms agreed with the appropriate reprographics rights organization. Enquiries concerning reproduction outside the scope of the above should be sent to the Rights Department, Oxford University Press, at the address above.

You must not circulate this work in any other form
and you must impose this same condition on any acquirer.

Published in the United States of America by Oxford University Press
198 Madison Avenue, New York, NY 10016, United States of America

British Library Cataloguing in Publication Data
Data available

Library of Congress Control Number: 2024950770

ISBN 9780198840947

DOI: 10.1093/9780192577689.001.0001

Printed and bound by
CPI Group (UK) Ltd, Croydon, CR0 4YY

Links to third party websites are provided by Oxford in good faith and
for information only. Oxford disclaims any responsibility for the materials
contained in any third party website referenced in this work.

The manufacturer's authorised representative in the EU for product safety is
Oxford University Press España S.A. of El Parque Empresarial San Fernando
de Henares, Avenida de Castilla, 2 – 28830 Madrid (www.oup.es/en or product.
safety@oup.com). OUP España S.A. also acts as importer into Spain of products
made by the manufacturer.

# CONTENTS

| | |
|---|---|
| *Preface* | *ix* |
| *Permissions* | *xiii* |
| I. The Bird in Glee: On the Nonsemantic | 1 |
| II. The Seasons: Paradigm of Lyric Time | 27 |
| III. Motion and Turn: Water's Ways | 57 |
| IV. The Imperceptible, or Wilderness | 85 |
| *Notes* | 109 |
| *Works Cited* | 129 |
| *Index* | 139 |

# PREFACE

In our time, there seems to me no more urgent critical task than the one that will reframe our relation to nature, going beyond subject–object dichotomies and asking what human practices tell us about our natural being and its situation among beings. My focus here is "poetry's nature." By this, I hope to indicate some essential aspects of poetry and as well the long tradition of apprehending natural phenomena through the work of poems. My examples are drawn largely, but not exclusively, from English tradition. As I have been thinking over the last several years about the history of what we call the nature poem, I've come to realize that we might go deeper into questions of the nature of poetry itself. What interests me are such simple questions as "how do I know I am experiencing a poem?" "what is a poetic line?" "what is a poetic image?" "what are we measuring when we speak of poetic meter or feeling when we speak of poetic rhythm?" When we consider our use of language for aesthetic ends, we immediately find we are in a living relation to other species and that our uses of beauty, like theirs, embed us within the animate world.

These four pieces explore some particular aspects of poetry's creation and reception: the ways poems veer between language and sound, and hence between semantic density and meaninglessness; the experience of seasonality as a paradigm for the lyric's recursive use of time; the flows and forms of water as an inspiration for the enactment and depiction of motion and rest

# PREFACE

in poems; and, finally, the vast domain of the imperceptible as a resource for the imagination. These concerns reach back to some of my earliest interests in poetics—in nonsense, in scale and significance, in the role of the human senses in the history of poetry—yet they are not meant to be a summation of any kind. This is a small volume addressing some very large questions within the confines of my expertise and my aim has been to think aloud about the topic and to encourage further scholarship by others.

These are lectures in two senses of the word: they are readings of a number of English poems and they were delivered to an audience as the Clarendon Lectures in English Literature at the University of Oxford in May, 2023. The audience was present in person and there was no recording. In preparing this volume I have changed very little of the original texts, but I have added notes in the hope they will be helpful.

I am grateful to the Oxford Faculty of English for their invitation and, once I arrived, for their engaging conversation and warm hospitality. I especially would like to thank the chair, Marion Turner, who graciously oversaw every aspect of my visit. Matthew Bevis, Erica McAlpine, Jennifer Gosetti-Ferencei, Santanu Das, Helen Small, Ankhi Mukherjee, Rachel Burns, Isobel Armstrong, Gwyneth Lewis, and, from Oxford University Press, Eleanor Collins all offered thoughts and suggestions that have been a great help to me. Conversations and correspondence with Jan Zwicky and Jay Wright in recent years have influenced my work here deeply, as has their own writing on the concerns of this study. My thinking has been enriched as well by weekly discussions with the graduate students in my final seminar at Princeton, a course on this topic in the Autumn of 2022. Jessica Brofsky from

PREFACE

my home department patiently helped me assemble my slides
before I left for England. Emily Lobb, also from Princeton, aided
me extensively with the last steps in preparing the manuscript.
Justin Bradshaw's drawings of water, one of which now appears
on and in this volume, have been a continuing inspiration.

# PERMISSIONS

"The Course of a Particular" is licensed from "Opus Posthumous" from *The Collected Poems of Wallace Stevens*, copyright © 1954 by Wallace Stevens and copyright renewed 1982 by Holly Stevens. Used by permission of Alfred A. Knopf, an imprint of the Knopf Doubleday Publishing Group, a division of Penguin Random House LLC. All rights reserved.

Images from Chantilly, Bibliothèque du Musée Condé, *Les Très Riches Heures du Duc de Berry*, MS 65 (October and November): cliché CNRS-IRHT, © Bibliothèque du Musée Condé, Château de Chantilly.

"Judith, or Cowper's Oak: A Portrait from Nature" drawn by Mrs. [Margaret] Meen, 1804, engraved by Caroline Watson, 1805, published 1806 by J. Seagrave for J. Johnson, Chichester, in William Hayley, "Supplementary pages to the Life of Cowper: containing the additions made to that work on reprinting it in octavo." Image obtained from Princeton University Rare Books. Public domain.

"r-p-o-p-h-e-s-s-a-g-r" copyright 1935 © 1963, 1991 by the Trustees for the e.e. cummings Trust. Copyright © 1978 by George James Firmage, from *Complete Poems: 1904–1962* by e. e. cummings, edited by George J. Firmage. Used by permission of Liveright Publishing Corporation.

"Poem (As the cat)" by William Carlos Williams, from *The Collected Poems: Volume 1, 1909–1939*, copyright © 1938 by New

PERMISSIONS

Directions Publishing Corp. Reprinted by permission of New Directions Publishing Corp.

"A light exists in Spring" and "Faith is a Fine Invention" by Emily Dickinson are reprinted from *The Poems of Emily Dickinson: Variorum Edition*, edited by Ralph W. Franklin, Cambridge, MA: The Belknap Press of Harvard University Press, copyright © 1998 by the President and Fellows of Harvard College. Copyright © 1951, 1955 by the President and Fellows of Harvard College. Copyright © renewed 1979, 1983 by the President and Fellows of Harvard College. Copyright © 1914, 1918, 1919, 1924, 1929, 1930, 1932, 1935, 1937, 1942 by Martha Dickinson Bianchi. Copyright © 1952, 1957, 1958, 1963, 1965 by Mary L. Hampson. Used by permission. All rights reserved.

Excerpt from "The Storm (*Forio d'Ischia*)" by Theodore Roethke: copyright © 1961 by Beatrice Roethke, Administratrix of the Estate of Theodore Roethke. Copyright © 1966 and renewed 1994 by Beatrice Lushington; from *Collected Poems by Theodore Roethke*. Used by permission of Doubleday, an imprint of the Knopf Doubleday Publishing Group, a division of Penguin Random house LLC. All rights reserved.

Permission for the use of "A Grave" is granted by the Literary Estate of Marianne C. Moore, David M. Moore, Esq., Successor Executor. All rights reserved.

# I

# THE BIRD IN GLEE: ON THE NONSEMANTIC

We speak of "our place in nature," but in truth there is no other place for us. Despite the foundation of Western thought in binaries between nature and culture, nature and the supernatural, and nature and mind, we have no broad agreement about the idea of nature or the role of human creativity within nature. In many cultures, including those of China and Japan, a notion of nature in general is not so much absent as simply irrelevant. For others, the Western problem of a diremption between nature and artifice is also beside the point.[1] I take these differences not so much as an opportunity to convert or transform Western attitudes toward nature, but rather as an indication that our thought about nature is part of a larger process of anthropomorphizing ourselves and taking responsibility for our powers, including our history of claims over space, time, and other creatures.

*Poetry's Nature.* Susan Stewart, Oxford University Press. © Susan Stewart (2025).
DOI: 10.1093/9780192577689.003.0001

Let me first review some of the historical context that strikes me as relevant to these questions—particularly those philosophical positions that have yoked practices of poetic making to processes of nature. By the fifth century BC, the Greek term for nature, *physis*, was inseparably bound to concepts of genesis or origin and the innate or characteristic aspects of being. For the pre-Socratics, nature became a technical term indicating the permanent and intrinsic qualities of matter. And from this beginning in notions of realism, or mind-independent existence, a distinction appears between such intrinsic qualities and what we perceive.[2]

A concern with matter, permanence, and time continues into Plato's thoughts on Forms, their instantiating particulars, and the enduring receptacle he proposes in the *Timaeus* as the origin and location of all that is coming to be.[3] He writes in the *Sophist* of the secondary work of human makers: "the things said (to be) by nature are made by a divine art, and the things put together by human beings out of these are made by a human art, and so in accordance with this speech I'll set down two genera of the art of making, one human and one divine."[4] And in the *Timaeus* he frames how human makers participate in divine creation by their work of generating likenesses. This work emerges and vanishes in time, which is itself "a moving image of eternity"—that eternity always in the background of the world of appearances. Pierre Hadot has written in his own history of the idea of nature of how these ideas linked poetic making to theologies of creation: "Since earliest antiquity, the poet has been thought to be the true interpreter of nature, who knew its secrets precisely insofar as it was imagined that nature acts like a poet, and that what nature produces is a poem." Hadot describes the *Timaeus* itself as a poem imitating the artistry of the great poem of the universe.[5]

In the compilation of Aristotle's lectures on nature that we call in English his *Physics*, he considers motion and life in relation to the transformation of matter and forces of causality. And to the extent that he also distinguishes between those natural things that grow and die and those artificial things that are destined by their matter and forms to certain outcomes, Aristotle as well considers the role of intention and purpose in the emergence of things.[6] In the *Nicomachean Ethics*, he writes that art in general, as the systematic exercise of human skill, "partly imitates nature and partly carries to completion what nature has left incomplete."[7] When we see in poems a language of nature or see in nature a symbolic alphabet or hieroglyphs, we are further participating in the excess, the superfluidity of meaning, that nature draws upon and toward which it draws us.

An emphasis upon nature as created and its relation to human making continues, too, in the thought of Aquinas and, later, Spinoza. Both distinguished between *natura naturans* and *natura naturata*. The first, *natura naturans*, is a self-formed nature that acts and creates. The second, *natura naturata*, indicates the individual forms of created nature, those particular manifestations of nature's processes.[8] According to this frame, observing the forms of *natura naturata*, we can infer those principles by which *natura naturans* operates—principles manifested in mathematics and proportion. This notion of ever-emerging phenomena linked through underlying patterns—whether such patterns are principles of geometry or what we call laws of nature—speaks to one way that an Aristotelian observational means of knowing constantly is brought up against a Platonic metaphysic.

The distinction between the intrinsic qualities of things in themselves and what we perceive famously persisted in Kant's separation of the noumenal from the phenomenal.[9] For Kant we humans remain within the phenomenal, for that is our world, the limit of our perception. Such a bifurcation of nature, or, as Alfred North Whitehead would later term it, such a "fallacy of misplaced concreteness," would not be fully put into question until the contributions of early twentieth-century physics and its companion, Whitehead's own process philosophy.[10] Whitehead went some distance in overcoming this fallacy by taking Kant's notion of the phenomenal all the way and claiming that nature is what we are aware of in perception. Or to phrase that in reverse: what we are aware of in perception is what nature is.[11]

Whitehead draws from Kant's critique of the power of judgment with its description of the suspension of the concept in the apprehension of beauty. In Whitehead's formulation our perception is an interplay of the pure sensual immediacy posed by those phenomena we encounter and our sense of causal relatedness—that is, our intuition of the relatedness of all nature—what Whitehead calls "the togetherness of things."[12] As Whitehead rejected the notion of an underlying material substrata for nature, he called for a recognition that the world is organic, rather than material. The development of later, and especially recent, science along lines that in fact modulate the boundary between the organic and the inorganic helps us understand that a comprehensive account of nature would bring together attempts to understand human psychology and teleology with attempts to understand modern physics.[13]

Whitehead continued the long critique of atomism initiated by Aristotle in arguing that nature is not atoms in a void, but a temporally experienced structure of mutually related "evolving processes." The contemporary physicist Carlo Rovelli similarly has argued that all reality lies "in the relations between physical systems." It isn't that things enter into relation, he says, "but rather that *relations* ground the notion of a *thing*."[14] Such a quantum frame for nature reminds us not only of the entangled relations between all things, but that perception, too, is a process amid processes and that we are perpetually engaged in creating forms and meanings out of our apprehension of, and engagement with, the world.

Whitehead, in fact, was the first writer to use the term *creativity* in a general sense.[15] This sense of creativity as the driving force of both matter and consciousness descends from these many earlier attempts to place human making within natural processes. Whitehead traced his thoughts on process to his immersion in the poetry of Wordsworth and other Romantics. From Wordsworth he took the notion of nature as a totality and a mysterious presence surrounding and shaping us to such an extent that we belong to it and become part of it. From Shelley he drew on a sense of nature as perpetual flux: changing, dissolving, transforming.[16] His homage might seem a matter of claiming cultural affinity alone, but Whitehead also was especially interested in what he called "non-uniform objects"—an example for him was a tune or poem or any event that is perceived as a whole via a certain duration. "Duration happens and passes," he says.[17] The structure we create as an unfolding poem is affected by the phenomenon to hand and yokes its duration to the duration of that phenomenon much as a wave is perceived as an immanent emergence.

The poet is inhabited by rhythm and compelled by sound as well as by an intention to mean; the poet is speaking in the deictic now and moving into the future. Always felt and not merely thought, poetry cannot be paraphrased or translated into concepts and remain poetry. In this regard, poetry, involving all our senses and bodily rhythms and produced in a process that employs more than the conscious will, is a practice that offers a more capacious means of knowledge than the exercise of reason alone. In other words, poetry deeply involves and arises from our embodied being. Furthermore, whereas the history of poetry mirrors changes in the history of cultural attitudes toward our sense of nature, poetic forms can powerfully set out and shape such changes. As I'll explore in my last lecture, a poem also might reveal in time the relation between what is outside of our perceptual and linguistic powers as it comes under those powers. This possibility obviously raises questions about traditions of the sublime and the differences between the productive and reproductive imagination. What we frame as the noumenal is not only intuited as other, but as well as an event on its way to happening.

When we consider the designation "nature poems" most broadly, we usually look for poems that name natural phenomena, or describe such phenomena, considering them as a mirror of human states, or talk "to" such phenomena, as with odes and apostrophes. Some poems are concerned with nature as a totality, some with particular events, patterns, forms, and objects. The nature poem per se has a history dating, so far as I know, to the

Egyptian Middle Kingdom religious hymns to the gods of wind and the sun and the Chinese Shi-ching *Book of Songs* from the eleventh to seventh centuries BCE—so often taking into consideration the cosmic year, the passing of the seasons, and weather.[18] We have a long-enduring, ever-evolving history of Western genres of nature poetry as well: the alba, the nocturne, the idyll, the pastoral, the eclogue, the georgic, and the topographical poem, each of which is tied to a means of human life and sociality—be it herding, subsistence farming, mating, or mercantilism. Yet if we attempt to situate human speakers fully within the nature of which they are a part, then every poem is a nature poem.

Poetry is always bound up with both the abstractions of cosmology and the embodiment of animal existence. If animal consciousness has been purged from metaphysics, it continues in the language of poetry. Opening the scale of time and envisioning other trajectories and other worlds are, too, ways of escaping the conventions of plot teleology and pre-determination. And the pursuit of an art practice that continually reformulates its own rules out of its materials—that is, language—evokes the possibility that even the universal laws of matter may be objects of historical transformation, as they have proved to be under the frames of chaos theory and the quantum revolution.

To think about the ways poems continually approach the frontiers of intelligibility, moving between pure sound and the most profound powers of symbolization, we might turn to the earliest recorded English-language poems available and those that reach to oral tradition. There we find a striking recurrence of what we might call nonsemantic devices. To clarify, by using the term "nonsemantic" I remember that anything without meaning is in a relation to meaning and thereby a means of underscoring the prevalence of meaning. In this way even meaninglessness is a kind of meaning. But the intentional interruption of reference nevertheless is of a different order than the lapse of intersubjective meaning that we find when we simply don't hear or understand one another. And such an interruption is indicative of the force of the emotional expression underlying all communication, regardless of its particular functions in context.

The most common of the nonsemantic devices I have in mind are the uses of rhythm and rhyme to organize the units of utterance rather than the orders of cause, sequence, and consequence alone. In two important essays from the mid-twentieth century,[19] W. K. Wimsatt pursued what he thought of as the alogical counterpattern that poetry places upon discursive meaning. Perhaps he took his clue from Percy Shelley's *Defence of Poetry*, where Shelley had claimed "Poetry ... differs from logic, that it is not subject to the controul of the active powers of the mind, and that its birth and recurrence has no necessary connexion with consciousness or will."[20] Yet unlike Shelley, with his speculations regarding the sources of poetic inspiration, Wimsatt worked as a formalist and described features of verbal art that are relational within the structure rather than referential to the world. The poetic, he contended, was the key practice distanced from logical prose discourse. He thereby called this practice "counterlogical." He specified first of all the phonetic repetitions (and semantic diremptions) of the pun, citing W. H. Auden's phrase from *The Poet's Tongue* that a pun is an "auditory metaphor." Wimsatt's list of forms included as well rhyme, alliteration, turn, and agnomination [a pun that involves a reframing, as in: "Small and bald Mr. Smith was in fact quite a big wig"]. He also mentions how

THE BIRD IN GLEE: ON THE NONSEMANTIC

"the equalities of meter ... cut across the parallels of sense." As opposed to discourses of logic, argument, and narrative, the poetic, Wimsatt held, is its own means of meaning. And he acknowledged dialectically that, in calling attention to itself and that different "reality which it resembles and symbolizes," the poetic both reminds us of that reality and asks us to consider what we have made.[21]

Wimsatt's argument is broad, but perhaps not as broad as it might be if we turn to more examples. I propose that we look more closely at internal effects of the nonsemantic within some individual works. I suggest this because the poetry we think of as foundational to the English tradition often makes a clear demarcation within the work between referential and self-referential language and between narrative and the deictic "now" of lyric utterance. And this self-referential language often evokes sounds and utterances from beyond intelligible, and even human, speech. Onomatopoetic representations of animal calls, and situating animal behavior in its hour and season, have long been features of poetry, and representations of birdsong are especially prevalent in late medieval and early modern work.

Here for example, is the poem we call "Sumer is icumen in," a widely anthologized thirteenth-century song that I'm sure is familiar, for it has become a point of origin for many accounts and anthologies of English lyric while also playing a continuing and vibrant role in the culture. The song is believed to be part of a commonplace book kept by the monks at Reading Abbey. The four/three form of the poem, a meter associated later with early modern ballads, is organized into a rota or round. It is written for four voices and two bass voices sing the ground.

9

POETRY'S NATURE

Sumer is icumen in
Lhude sing cuccu
Groweþ sed
and bloweþ med
and springþ þe wde nu
Sing cuccu

Awe bleteþ after lomb
lhouþ after calue cu
Bulluc sterteþ
bucke uerteþ
murie sing cuccu

Cuccu cuccu
Wel singes þu cuccu
ne swik þu nauer nu

Sing cuccu nu
Sing cuccu
Sing cuccu
Sing cuccu nu

In this lyric, the imperative to sing, "Sing cuckoo," is directed to the cuckoo, demanding at once that the bird sing his song and that the song itself sounds "cuckoo," and as well to the human singer who is singing the song of the cuckoo. That is, the singer can at once spur on herself, her companions in singing, and the bird. The European cuckoo, *cuculus canorus*, sings something close to a cuc-coo in actuality and does so in myriad French, Italian, and German cuckoo songs as well.

The context of the imperative is an expanding scene of fertility—the first stanza scales out from seed to meadow to wood (growing, blooming, and budding); the second from female ewe and cow (bleating, lowing) to male bull and billy goat (prancing,

## THE BIRD IN GLEE: ON THE NONSEMANTIC

farting). As these animals have their motions, so do the cuckoo and the human, who exercise their power of song. Yet the cuckoo lays its eggs in the nests of other birds and is associated in folk song and legend with both adultery and orphanage. At the end of Shakespeare's *Love's Labour's Lost*, for example, the owl's song, to wit, to woo, is associated with winter and fidelity, whereas the cuckoo's song presents [a] "word of fear / Unpleasing to a married ear" (5.2.984–5). And the bird evokes further associations: like the owl and the crow, the cuckoo sings only its name rather than a true song—a kind of aural selfie. The cuckoo and the nightingale traditionally announce the coming of spring. In much English folklore they arrive on the third of April.[22]

To the consternation of many scholars, however, in this lyric it is summer and not spring that is coming in: the animals already have borne their young and the world is in full flower.[23] The beginning of spring, as it always does, has begotten the beginning of summer and the singers are urged never to stop. Never stopping, in fact, is always an impossible possibility, a possible impossibility, in singing a round. The round begins and ends in a solo voice, hence poignantly in another sense of orphanage: abandonment or exhaustion rather than closure.

"Sumer is icumen in" is in so many ways a lyric of perpetual beginnings—the beginning of a season, the beginning of new life, the beginning of the song itself. It is structured, obviously not by narrative, but rather by anticipation. The frame is the immediacy of the here and now. Like other works built around the seasons— for now we can think of books of hours, the Scrovegni Chapel, or Haydn's oratorio based on James Thomson's masterpiece "The Seasons"—progression is pattern, a matter of felt correspondences rather than development toward closure. We feel the weather and changes in the weather on our skin. If we have ever found talk about the weather empty in the past, we certainly are not finding it so today.

At the same time, as I've hoped to indicate, our knowledge of natural patterns and forms often comes from poems and other works of art so much as from lived experience. When Descartes, for example, lists examples of what he thinks of as animal mechanisms—swallows returning in spring, honey bees maintaining their hives, cranes taking their annual flight—he draws on epic similes in the *Iliad* and the *Aeneid* and the descriptions registered in Virgil's *Georgics*.[24]

Furthermore, the human singing in "Summer is icumen in" may strike us as predominant, but it is useful to remember, as the biologist Heather Williams has explained, that vocal learning is rare among mammals. Only one primate species (we humans), the cetaceous species whales and dolphins, and two kinds of bats imitate vocal communication signals. But there are more than 4,000 species of birds that do so: the thirty-five to fifty-five families of songbirds or oscines. The oscines come to sing by learning: first by listening and memorizing, then by producing sounds and listening to the results, a kind of babbling; then by practicing songs; and finally by coming to knowledge as the song becomes stereotyped or fixed.[25] And some birds, for example mockingbirds and nightingales, demonstrate great *individual* variety in their songs, a variety that might be described as invention.

Birdsong thus develops through skills of listening and imitation as well as utterance. Young birds may learn from a parent bird or from another adult bird. A bird sings to mark its territory and to attract a mate. We sometimes distinguish between bird calls, which are used for immediately practical ends such as

## THE BIRD IN GLEE: ON THE NONSEMANTIC

indicating danger or direction, and birdsongs, typically longer and more complex communications that summon mates. Yet the sheer excess of birdsong also may indicate, as the late E. O. Wilson has suggested, that all species feel exuberance in the context of the flourishing beauty of the natural world.[26] Clearly in this lyric, human beings, too, are singing through a process of listening and imitation—of the cuckoo and of other human singers. And rhyme underscores the literal coincidence of the human song and the birdsong.

I will not attempt to explore the many parallel features of birdsong and human language. The extremely fast tempo and variability of birdsong, and the fact that we humans hear only a fraction of the actual sound in play, make any simple theory of imitation by human singing and music continue to be a vague and Romantic claim.[27] Yet recent research by the neurolinguist Erich Jarvis at Rockefeller University describes how those animals that have a capacity for vocal learning are also the only animals that can dance along to a precise musical beat. Although more than 300 million years separate us from a common ancestor, in our ability to imitate and reproduce sounds, we have more in common with songbirds, parrots, and hummingbirds than with chimpanzees; and these birds have more in common with us than they have with chickens. Jarvis hypothesizes that, in the process of evolution, we animals who can hear new sounds and reproduce them developed this skill as an innovation and specialization of our motor pathways. And a subset of these animals—humans and dolphins—are able to use their learned sounds for affective communication as well as semantics.[28]

For our purposes, we can turn to the fact that myriad poets have been drawn to transcribing or otherwise recording bird

POETRY'S NATURE

songs in, let's call them, human phonemes on the page. Gerard
Manley Hopkins's poem, "The Woodlark," begins:

> *Teevo cheevo cheevio chee:*
> O where, what can thát be?
> *Weedio-weedio*: there again!
> So tiny a trickle of sóng-strain
> And all round not to be found
> For brier, bough, furrow, or gréen ground
> Before or behind or far or at hand
> Either left either right
> Anywhere ín the súnlight.
> Well, after all! Ah but hark–
> 'I am the little woodlark. ...

The poem is based on an entry from June 3, 1866 in Hopkins's
journal where he wrote of the juxtaposition of bird songs: "The
cuckoo singing one side, on the other from the ground and
unseen the wood-lark, as I suppose, most sweetly with a song of
which the structure is more definite than the skylark's and gives
the link with that of the rest of the birds."[29]

Dating to a period thirty years earlier, John Clare's account
of his evolving relation to poetic sound, his "The Progress of
Rhyme," includes the poetic conventions of harp, lyre, talking
birds that "croak," and singing birds that "tweet,"[30] and gradually
claims a reciprocal relation between singer and listener: He
writes, "I heard the blackbird in the dell / Sing sweet could I but
sing as well / I thought until the bird in glee / Seemed pleased &
paused to answer me." This passage comes immediately before
his account of standing, as a boy, over an "old oak railing"
listening, as he said, for half a day to the song of a nightingale,
and he goes on to record that sound in syllables:

14

## THE BIRD IN GLEE: ON THE NONSEMANTIC

"Chew-chew chew-chew" & higher still
"Cheer-cheer cheer-cheer" more loud & shrill
"Cheer-up cheer-up cheer-up"—& dropt
Low "Tweet tweet jug jug jug" & stopt
One moment just to drink the sound
Her music made & then a round
Of stranger witching notes was heard
As if it was a stranger bird.
"Wew-wew wew-wew chur-chur chur-chur
"Woo-it woo-it"—could this be her
"Tee-rew tee-rew tee-rew tee-rew
"Chew-rit chew-rit"—& ever new
"Will-will will-will grig-grig grig-grig"
The boy stopt sudden on the brig
To hear the "tweet tweet tweet" so shrill
The "jug jug jug" & all was still
A minute—when a wilder strain
Made boys & woods to pause again
Words were not left to hum the spell
Could they be birds that sung so well—...[31]

This passage is justly celebrated as one of the most carefully transcribed accounts of birdsong in English tradition. Yet we should note that as he develops these lines from conventional croaks and tweets to a final unintelligible "wilder strain," Clare also carefully shows us the limits of anthropomorphism. The "wilder strain" cannot be represented in meaningful human phonemes, let alone in the imperatives of "cheer up" and "chew it."

Such a drift toward the limits of intelligibility in lyric form strikes me as important not only because it indicates a comparison, both negative and positive, between bird communication and human speech, but also because it is a recurring feature in the history of poetry. Like other aspects of poetry's "nature," it is

15

not merely a theme, but also a matter of practice, and not merely atavistic, but also a means, to use Ezra Pound's expression, to "make it new."

In a brilliant book published in 2012, Robert Stark described Pound's own indebtedness to birdsong as a method or technique in his early verse. Stark describes how Pound was drawn toward birdsong for its relation to music on the one hand and its opacity and obscurity on the other.[32] He explains that the word we often use for such obscurity, *jargon*, originally was a word indicating birdsong, reminding us of how Coleridge used the word in *The Rime of the Ancient Mariner*:

> Sometimes a-dropping from the sky
> I heard the sky-lark sing;
> Sometimes all little birds that are,
> How they seemed to fill the sea and air
> With their sweet jargoning!

Jargon evolves to include polyglot terms and other opaque words and phrases. Throughout his book, Stark recounts Pound's instruction in the jargon of the troubadours. In his early treatise *The Spirit of Romance* Pound particularly praises the resonance of bird sounds in the poetry of Arnaut Daniel and decades later, in his *ABC of Reading*, he was still marveling at Arnaut's mimetic skills: "[Arnaut had] made the birds sing IN HIS WORDS; I don't mean that he merely referred to the birds singing—. . . he kept them at it, repeating the tune, and finding five rhymes for each of the seventeen rhyme sounds in the same order. . . . Having done that he constructed another perfect strophe, where the bird call interrupts the verse. . . . That again for six strophes WITH the words making sense."[33]

## THE BIRD IN GLEE: ON THE NONSEMANTIC

In Pound's own translations of Arnaut, he maintains these bird sound transcriptions, as in the opening of "Doutz Brais e Critz," which he renders as "Sweet cries and cracks":

> Sweet cries and cracks
> and lays and chants inflected
> By auzels who, in their Latin belikes,
> Chirm each to each, even as you and I
> Pipe toward those girls on whom our thoughts attract ...[34]

As Stark and other scholars have noted, Pound is immersed here in Arnaut not only as a master of sound, but also as an emblematic voice of polyglottism. In the *Commedia*, Purgatorio 26, Dante had preserved Arnaut's Provençal and that switch from Tuscan can be placed beside a panoply of the *Commedia*'s polyglot expressions: Cacciaguida and the angels speak Latin, Nimrod speaks nonsense, Bonagiunta speaks Lucchese dialect, Caccianemico speaks Bolognese slang, and so on.

This kind of mixture of natural sounds and varied languages characterizes the intellectual milieu of much medieval lyric between 800 and 1300 and continues on in the oral tradition even into the present. We find it, for example, in the choruses of many Child ballads.[35] It can be as simple as "Fa la la la, fa la la la ra re," which can be found in "Riddles wisely expounded" (Child Ballad 1) and "Sing ohon, ohon, and ohon O / ... / Adown by the greenwode side O" found in "The Cruel Mother" (CB 20), and the variant "Lady Anne." We also find it in the sounds offered up by counting out rhymes, such as, from my own childhood, "Harum scarum / Virgin marum / out go you."

17

## POETRY'S NATURE

Here are some further examples from ballad refrains, starting with this version of the many songs and lullabies derived from the riddle format of Child ballads 1 and 46:

> I had four brothers over the sea,
> *Perry merry dinctum dominee;*
> And each one sent a present unto me;
> *Partum, quartum, perry dee centum,*
> *Perry merry dinctum dominee.*

Here we have a jumble slightly evocative of Latin and Greek: *peri* as *around*; *partum* as *create*; *quartum* as *fourth*; *centum* as *one hundred*.

Consider, too, this Kentucky version of "Sir Lionel" where we find more "semi-Latin":

> There is a wild boar in these woods,
> *Dillom dom dillom.*
> He eats our flesh and drinks our blood,
> *Tum a qui quiddle quo qum.*[36]

Are these fragments of a lost, no longer functioning, ritual language? As terms that resist use or subordination to theme, they remain expressions of the purely emotive or aesthetic unto themselves.

The nonsemantic refrain also can use ordinary English words. Here is a sample you might recognize from "The Twa Corbies" (CB 26). Proceeding by incremental repetition, this profound and tragic ballad is concerned in many ways with mirroring language between the animal and human worlds as it explores relations between fertility, birth, human burial practices, and death:

> Down there comes a fallow doe
> *Down a down, hay down, hay down*

18

THE BIRD IN GLEE: ON THE NONSEMANTIC

As great with young as she might go,
*With a down,*
Down there comes a fallow doe
As great with young as she might go
*With a down derry, derry, derry, down, down.*

In these refrains, often called nonsense refrains, a voice from outside comes breaking in. It might be the voice of the social, the choral, the adjacent, or, as with Clare's poem, the wild and unintelligible. The folk song scholar Bess Lomax Hawes thought the nonsense refrains in lullabies reinforced the vowel sounds and permutations of the vowel sounds of the parent (in every sense!) language. She and her colleagues frequently found patterns of preferred phonemes in the use of nonsense syllables and humming, with basic patterns of assonance particularly evident in those lullabies. Alan Lomax and Edith Trager had discovered that in Spain vowel preferences were implanted by mothers in their children during infancy. Bess Hawes in turn found that whereas many kinds of songs are sung as lullabies, lullabies also are typically sung without words and that nonsense syllables, such as "dee dee" or "na na" are used rather than strict humming. Indeed, in Italian, lullabies are called "Ninna-nanni."

Regional and subcultural patterning recurs in nonsense refrains of all genres of folk songs and interaction with infants often involves shifting between chats and lulls—that is, vocalizing versus making repetitive comforting noises.[37] These practices take us continually to the border between understanding and incomprehension that we once knew so well as we ourselves first encountered language. And they remind us of the force of emotion and music underlying expressive speech.

POETRY'S NATURE

Some refrains of this type are nonsemantic on the level of the word, others on the level of the phrase: the well-known refrain "Parsley, sage, rosemary, and thyme" was probably a medical formula with an arbitrary relation to the theme of the work. In his study of this refrain, the folklorist Roger Abrahams made this list of its variations:

> Save rosemary and thyme.
> Rosemary in time.
> Every rose grows merry in time.
> Rose de Marian Time.
> Rozz marrow and time.
> May every rose bloom merry in time.
> Let every rose grow merry and fine.
> Every leaf grows many a time.
> Sing Ivy leaf, Sweet William and thyme.
> Every rose grows bonny in time.
> Every globe grows merry in time.
> Green grows the merry antine.
> Whilst every grove rings with a merry antine.
> So sav'ry was said, come marry in time.[38]

The technical point is that the structure of birdsong imitation, like our use of nonsense refrains, calls on our phonology rather than our syntax. The latter arises from our capacity to create meaningful utterances in sequences and to embed them within one another and place them in a recursive relationship. It also demonstrates our ability to generate entirely new phrasing. These powers stand, so far as we know, in sharp contrast to the signals and songs of birds and other nonhuman species. In the case of polyglot or macaronic phrasing, what may have made syntactical sense is taken back into phonology, perhaps a kind of

# THE BIRD IN GLEE: ON THE NONSEMANTIC

atavistic babble. These moments of sung sound that punctuate and delay the progress of syntax seem to appear most frequently in songs of hunting and the animal world, birdsong and bird talk, love poems, songs to and for children, and other poems concerned with fertility and organic life in general.

Repetitive patterns of sounds, as we know from the work of Milman Parry and Albert Lord in their studies of Yugoslav epic performance,[39] give oral performers time to gather their thoughts for the next verse, strophe, or stanza. And because they are unvarying, they stand in contrast to any narrative development the intervening stanzas may present. Ballads in particular display the whole repertoire of sound production from vocalized musical or emotional utterance to meaningless phonemes to nonsemantic sequences of recognizable words. And in this it is important to underscore that the ballad singer is setting up not merely two parallel time systems, but as well, punctuating narrative time. The ballad often can be considered as displaying those features of poetic language that are compressed in lyric per se.

The nonsense refrain, the turn to "scat" or other sung wordless vocables, the obsessive repetition of vowel sounds, and imitation of visual forms of the kind we find in seventeenth-century poetry, the very notion that "the rhyme made me say it" or "the form demands it" all indicate a role for poetry beyond epistemology per se and intended expression. Just as the marking of territory in animal signification becomes expressive beyond mere function, the poem's space and time claim our attention as the sounds connect disparate circumstances.[40]

I have emphasized the premodern world of early lyrics where we hear distinctly both the relation between human and animal

21

utterance and their separation. Ezra Pound showed us that this issue, which is also a great resource, did not disappear in later poetry. Under a similar spirit of continuing traditions, let's look at one more Modernist poem together, but in this case one without direct reference to the troubadours or other early poetry. Here is "The Course of a Particular" by Wallace Stevens:

Today the leaves cry, hanging on branches swept by wind,
Yet the nothingness of winter becomes a little less.
It is still full of icy shades and shapen snow.
The leaves cry ... One holds off and merely hears the cry.

It is a busy cry, concerning someone else.
And though one says that one is part of everything,
There is a conflict, there is a resistance involved;
And being part is an exertion that declines:
One feels the life of that which gives life as it is.

The leaves cry. It is not a cry of divine attention,
Nor the smoke-drift of puffed-out heroes, nor human cry.
It is the cry of leaves that do not transcend themselves,
In the absence of fantasia, without meaning more
Than they are in the final finding of the ear, in the thing
Itself, until, at last, the cry concerns no one at all.[41]

The work appeared in *The Hudson Review* in the Spring of 1951 and a letter Stevens wrote to Robert Pack indicates that he inadvertently had left it out of his 1954 book *The Rock*.[42] The poem is a sustained act of attention. Its use of a refrain—"the leaves cry"—is an anomaly in Stevens's oeuvre. Yet, as I hope I've indicated, while refrains historically are a means of pulling the speaker away from the progress of the poem's action, here the refrain powerfully works as a summons back to the phenomenon at hand.

## THE BIRD IN GLEE: ON THE NONSEMANTIC

What is that phenomenon? It is the very sound of the refrain itself—the tentative anthropomorphism of the cry of the leaves. Not Stevens's objective "sound of the leaves" that goes all the way back thirty years to "The Snow Man" in *Harmonium*, but instead *a cry*—an outcome of a sentience stemming not from the hearer, but from the source: the hanging leaves.

The three opening lines juxtapose three different time schemes to the duration of this cry—the deictic today, and two paradoxical features of winter: its diminishing nothingness and its continuing, persistent forms of icy shades and shapen snow. The refrain of the cry appears again, followed by an ellipsis that is as well quite unusual in Stevens's work. The ellipsis creates both a blank and a pause, hearkening to its etymology as a "leaving out." On the other side of this blank or leaving out is a mandate of nonresponse, nonreciprocity between the anthropomorphized leaves and the human listeners: "One holds off and merely hears the cry." Yet on closer look, nonreciprocity is not exactly what is happening. "Holds off " is an expression we use when we imagine the course of weather—rain or snow will "hold off " and not fall. As the leaves mimic human intention, Stevens's "one" mimics the withholding of nature. One merely hears and does not respond to the cry.

Lines 5–9 pull away from the immediacy of the situation to reflect upon it. The speaker concludes that this is a busy cry concerning someone else—that is, not the speaker. The busy cry of the leaves is involved in, it *has*, a "purposive purpose," as Kant has framed the problem. That is, it has an intention unavailable to the human hearer. The speaker's realization here that he is overhearing as well as hearing evokes the paradigmatic situation of the reader who hears and overhears whenever a speech situation is represented in a poem.

At mid-poem, the speaker draws conclusions: "though one says that one is part of everything, there is a conflict, there is a resistance involved; and being part is an exertion that declines; one feels the life of that which gives life as it is." A course is a movement or flow that continues unimpeded; the course of a particular is to be merged into the whole, for the *natura naturata* to be taken back into its source in the *natura naturans*. As the nothingness of winter becomes a little less, every particular is itself due to its resistance to being something else—a detail, a shape, a form, an essence. Nevertheless, all living things are part of entropy, the exertion that declines until death and the reabsorption back into life as it is.

The poem clearly could end there, at the end of particularity. But Stevens reintroduces the cry. And he begins to distinguish it from what it is not. What it is not is an array of cultural forms: the divine, the heroic, and the human. The speaker paradoxically acknowledges the cry of leaves that "do not transcend themselves," that are in and for themselves, without fantasia and meaning. The cry is not the product of a human imagination, nor is it socially constructed, or intelligible beyond itself. The human ear can find or come upon this cry, and, without intention or volition, can hear this cry, but the thing itself, concerning no one at all, is part of a process that is not concerned with any "one." Nevertheless, the speaker cannot help but be preoccupied with what he imagines is the cry of the leaves—it remains a nonreciprocal concern, the limit of what can be thought and known.

With this introduction, I hope to have given you some sense of my own preoccupations with the nature and situation of poetry.

The meaning-making of all poems, the repository in many ways of our most continuous and deepest meanings, seems to draw on the origins of human language in the nonmeaning of pure sound and musicality. These examples of poetry's liminal powers show us poetry's role as a continuing paradigm of creativity—a creativity so often responding to creation.

# II

# THE SEASONS: PARADIGM OF LYRIC TIME

In my first lecture, I asked about the qualities of poetic form and what distinguishes poetry from discursive prose. Specifically, I aimed to explore how poems come under the shaping forces of nonsemantic features of language: the pulse of rhythm and measures of meter that cut and form poetic lines, the acoustic coincidences of rhymes and puns, and the pure sound play that we find so often in refrains. In the nonsense choruses of ballads, we could see vividly how nonsemantic interludes interrupt narrative progression. I would like to turn now more deeply to how, within the broad array of verbal art, time in lyric poetry is distinguished from, and indeed how it often markedly departs from, narrative in general. In order to do that, I'll begin, rather counterintuitively, by surveying some features of chronology and narrative, for I believe these features put the experience of lyric temporality in relief.

Our starting point might again be Aristotle. This time, let's turn to his comments in the *Poetics* on the differences between

*Poetry's Nature.* Susan Stewart, Oxford University Press. © Susan Stewart (2025).
DOI: 10.1093/9780192577689.003.0002

poetry and history writing. There he contends that poetry is more serious and more philosophical than history and, further, that whereas history speaks in particulars, poetry speaks in universals.[1] The implication is that speaking of universals is more serious and more philosophical than speaking of particulars—at least in part because universals recur and particulars are fleeting.

His statement thereby invites us to consider that history and poetry involve quite different orders of time and action, for what is particular happens as a single event and what is universal happens repeatedly. If narrative speaks in moments that move us to remember and recount, those are the particulars we experience as significant marks in the flow of otherwise unmarked time. If poetry speaks in universals, those are the universals we find not in abstractions alone, but also in repetition, in the turn of the seasons, the processes of organic life, decay, and reemergence, and through the reciprocating calls and responses in which all living things participate. And we remember that not only chronology, but also our sense of the span of our existence and of temporality itself, are rooted in such processes and not vice versa.

We don't have to be shepherds following calendars or farmers following almanacs to be aware of the interrelation of seasonal changes in the life cycles of biological organisms. Noting changes in the lives of plants and animals, we can observe the onset of what we think of as times of year, changes in the seasons, ends, and beginnings. And, bereft of mechanical aids, we human beings can tell time more finely by looking at the position of the sun or the length and position of our own shadows, turning ourselves into sundials. Another means of telling time appears in John Clare's lyric "Clock a Clay," where he alludes to telling the time by means of ladybugs. According to Northamptonshire folklore,

## THE SEASONS: PARADIGM OF LYRIC TIME

there were several methods: reading the number of spots on the ladybug's back as the time,[2] placing a ladybug on the back of your hand and numbering hours as you say "fly away home," or counting "hours" by tapping your foot to numbers until she flies away. This is the poem:

**Clock a Clay**

1
In the cowslips peeps I lye
Hidden from the buzzing fly
While green grass beneath me lies
Pearled wi' dew like fishes eyes
Here I lye a clock a clay,
Waiting for the time o' day

2
While grassy forests quake surprise
And the wild wind sobs and sighs
My gold home rocks as like to fall
On its pillars green and tall
When the pattering rain drives bye
Clock a clay keeps warm and dry

3
Day by day and night by night
All the week I hide from sight
In the cowslips peeps I lye
In rain and dew still warm and dry
Day and night and night and day
Red black spotted clock a clay

4
My home it shakes in wind and showers
Pale green pillar top't wi' flowers

POETRY'S NATURE

Bending at the wild winds breath
Till I touch the grass beneath
Here still I live lone clock a clay
Watching for the time of day[3]

Clare has written a dramatic monologue in tetrameter couplets that move liltingly between trochees and iambs—speaking and singing in the voice of the ladybug herself. The ladybug tells us about her surroundings in great detail: under the petals of the cowslip and above the green grass she is safe from predators and weather. The worst that can happen is the possibility of being knocked down into the grass. And what is she doing? Day by day and night by night all the week she hides from sight; day and night and night and day, she's "watching for the time of day"—the very information human beings derive from her. Clare wonderfully inverts the human desire to tell time by nature by having nature tell time in human terms.

Even so, as we know from "once upon a time," we exist within particulars and moments. The universals of philosophy are products of reflection upon experience and lyric poetry especially, as it begins in the *now* of utterance and emerges through recursive turns, often demonstrates the work of reflection itself. In contrast, narrative, including history writing, most often has been concerned with the singularity of events and the cascade of their consequences. We use narrative to shape our sense of what has happened and what matters. With narrative we rearrange sequence and details. Narrative time is both sequential and kairotic. The teleology of plot shapes our sense of consequence regarding the matter of narrative and leads, in denouement and closure, to the construction of meaning. Moments of narrative reflection and reflexivity, metanarrative designs arising from the practice of writing itself, underscore significance, but do not change the underlying order of events.

In these senses, narrative is implicitly bound to techniques of causal explanation. It is shaped by prior knowledge and by the organization of detail under such knowledge. We often give priority to firsthand testimony or witnessing, for example, yet a participant in an action, or even a participant observer, may be among the most unreliable of narrators. The narrator tries to answer, to suffice, and is driven by what is already known and by a sense of sequential inevitability—a sense that is especially vulnerable to irony because of the inherently limited perspectives of not only the actors within the story but also the narrator. The historian and theorist of historiography Hayden White described narration as such a "knowing account" in a 1972 essay: "The important point," he wrote, "is that in the concept 'narrative history' the literal meaning and usage direct attention, not to the 'story' being told as a 'fiction,' but to the knowledge-ability of the person telling the story. In short, literally speaking, the term 'narrative' qualifies the term 'history' in an *epistemological* not an aesthetic sense."[4]

We also recognize that the scope of an event can depend on the scope of narrative duration itself. In his unjustly neglected book on "the idea of nature," R. G. Collingwood spoke to this issue of scope in a passage worth quoting at length. "What is true," he writes, "of modern physics is a familiar feature of history. If an historian had no means of apprehending events that occupied more than an hour, he could describe the burning down of a house but not the building of a house; the assassination of Caesar but not his conquest of Gaul." He points out that "If two historians gave each his own answer to the question: 'What kinds of events happen, or can or might happen, in history?' their answers would be extremely different if one habitually thought of an event as something that takes an hour and the other as something that takes ten years; and a third who conceived an event as taking anything up to 1,000 years would give a different answer again.... The shorter our standard time-phase for an historical event," he says, "the more our history will consist of destructions, catastrophes, battles, murder, and sudden death. ... The natural processes that come most easily within ordinary human observation, it may be, are predominantly of a destructive kind."[5]

Lyric, in contrast, is one of the verbal forms that, absent narrative voice, frames events as aesthetic rather than solely epistemological. The poem is sensuously apprehended in time. The reader/listener is absorbed in it as it happens and through such devices as rhyme, recurring imagery, and refrain, is pulled back when moving forward, just as the intricacy of the work invites rereading, reexperiencing. Lyric time thus draws us in and as well invites us to reflect and seek out analogies, connections, resonances. It is agony to hear a joke we already know and yet a joy to hear again a beloved poem. The events of a poem unfold in what we think of as "real time" as experienced by a subject or subjects. This immersion in time is a feature of songs explained famously, for example, by Augustine in his *Confessions* where he writes, "Suppose that I am going to recite a psalm that I know. Before I begin, my faculty of expectation is engaged by the whole of it. But once I have begun, as much of the psalm as I have removed from the province of expectation and relegated to the past now engages my memory, and the scope of the action which

THE SEASONS: PARADIGM OF LYRIC TIME

I am performing is divided between the two faculties of memory and expectation ... What is true," he says, "of the whole psalm is also true of all its parts and of each syllable."[6]

Each poem pursues a nisus toward finality of form and, in its necessary imperfection, takes part in the stream of practices that is the ever unfinished, ever allusive and self-referential, project of making poems and living a life. Long before Keats put forward the importance of negative capability—a willingness to inhabit doubts, hesitations, and uncertainties—the practice of poetry has been committed to the emergence of knowledge rather than its representation and finality.

Poetry of course can take a narrative or retrospective form and narratives can use graphic devices, sound play, imagery, and other techniques that characterize poetry. Yet in all known genre systems, story and song seem to be distinct forms.[7] The person speaking or remembering the speech of the poem is feeling something as well as, or even at times rather than, knowing something. To extend the comparison further, whatever knowledge arrives at the end of the poem that was not known at the beginning of the poem has come from such feeling.

Just as birdsong offered us a paradigm for call and response and the many functions of imitation, fixed form, variation, sociality, and solo voice in human *poiesis*, so, we could say, do the seasons offer lyric a paradigm for pattern and variation in the experience of temporality. Northrop Frye went so far as to align each season with a literary genre: comedy with spring, romance with summer, tragedy with autumn, and satire with winter.[8] The seasons are changes not merely contemplated abstractly, as visual and auditory signs; as I noted in my first lecture, they are, like all weather, felt on the skin.

Regardless of altitude, specific weather patterns of wind and water temperature, geology, and topography, the seasons, like other cyclical and recursive forms, provide us with a frame for continuity and change at once. As patterns of weather, they are subject to flux and unpredictable beyond a certain purview of immediacy. They invite us to read signs external to human volition, yet they also are bound up with our own sense consciousness and cultural conventions, including calendars, festivals, ritual occasions, legends, and myths. Every living being comes under their dominion in time. Their resemblance is, as Gilles Deleuze noted of cycles in general, a qualitative judgment whereas their duration and measurable features are quantitative judgments.[9] In this they might help us grasp the tension between the qualitative sensation of poetic rhythm and the quantitative dimension of poetic meter.

Further, the meaning of *poiesis* as making, the production of form by means of effort, echoes the association in agricultural societies of the seasons with human labor. Such labor is a prominent theme of much of the seasonal pictorial imagery that many works of art both draw upon and codify: fires in winter, buds in spring, fruits in summer, fallen leaves in autumn. Consider two well-known depictions of seasonal labor from the fifteenth-century Duc du Berry's book of hours (see Figures 1 and 2). October is represented by plowing, and in the illustration for November, a swineherd is shaking down a crop of acorns for his waiting pigs. Striking as these images are, the interconnected and transformative aspects of the seasons, their verges, turns, and intensifications can be brought forward perhaps even more vividly by the temporality of verbal art.

**Figure 1** Paul Limbourg and Jean Colombe, "October" from "Les Très Riches Heures du Duc de Berry" MS 65 Musée Condé, Chantilly

**Figure 2** Jean Colombe, "November" from "Les Très Riches Heures du Duc de Berry" MS 65 Musée Condé, Chantilly

## THE SEASONS: PARADIGM OF LYRIC TIME

As these external experiences of time have profound effects upon the internal weather of our own emotions and well-being, they as well give us a sense of changes in pattern and patterns of changes that are intrinsic to poetic form. In the Western world, at least since the invention of agriculture and the notions of an Edenic first and a post-Edenic second nature, poetry has been bound up with a temporal sense based in the experience of living under the seasons and finding the means of life within and against the necessity of change. Just as breath is at the center of concepts of inspiration, the expansions of spring and summer and contractions of autumn and winter inform the relation between anticipation and intensification in poetic forms themselves (what Goethe called *steigerung*).[10] The earthly seasons can be given set dates of commencement according to the solstices, but they will not conform to such dicta from the heavens; an idea of resemblance is necessary to follow their progression as they fade into the next season, making early appearances or late farewells or suddenly reemerging. They can be "unseasonable" because we hold to their revolving succession. As we saw with "Sumer is icumen in," the fertility of plant and animal life is a subject of celebration, and those poems that have survived from the ancient and medieval worlds are replete with such celebrations, descriptions of changing weather, and accounts of tasks that need to be completed. They call to mind our sense of mating seasons, birthing seasons, hunting seasons, and harvest.

Marcel Mauss concluded in his study of seasonal variations in the lives of Eskimo people, "we have only to observe what goes on around us in our western societies to discover these same rhythms. ... we have come upon a law that is probably of considerable generality. Social life does not continue at the same level throughout the year; it goes through regular, successive phases of increased and decreased intensity, of activity and repose, of exertion and recuperation." Mauss held that these patterns of withdrawal and reanimation were intrinsic to the rhythm of human sociability and that the seasons, rather than functioning as determining causes of such rhythm, were instead greeted as the most appropriate contexts for changes in religion, festivity, law, and moral life.[11]

Western poetry is perhaps far behind the great sophistication of traditions like the Japanese *haiku*, which always suggests a particular season, and the accompanying practice of the *haiga*, painted images and calligraphy regarding the seasons, and the *kigo*, which attaches specific seasons to specific images—spring with skylarks, frogs, and cherry blossoms; summer with cicadas, wisteria, and southern winds; autumn with crickets, persimmons, and bright leaves; winter with oysters, fallen leaves, and icicles.[12] Yet in the initiation rites of the Eleusinian mysteries, the stories of Demeter and Persephone, the spill of turns and negations, from creation to destruction, in *Ecclesiastes* 3, with Passover pilgrims to the Temple of Jerusalem, the traditions of Christ as a gardener, and conventional associations of the seasons with the four humors, Western poetry, too, has found depth and significance in the experience of seasonality.

When we think of the *natureingang* or nature introduction, most often celebrating spring and bird songs, at the start of so many *cansos* and *sirventes* in Occitan poetry we find the scene can either spark the immediacy and urgency of the poet's speech, as it does in Guiraut de Bornelh's "Can lo freitz e·l glatz e la neus" (When the ice and cold and snow retreat) or Arnaut's "Can chai la fueilla" (When sere leaf falleth) where the cold season cannot quench the lover's ardor. Or the changing season can serve as a contrast to the speaker's sorrow, as it does in Bernart de Ventadorn's "Can l'erba 'fresch'" (When tender grass and leaves appear), as spring only underscores the speaker's suffering.[13] We find this contrast in English in "Foweles in the frith":

> Foweles in the frith,
> The fisses in the flod,
> And I mon waxe wod.
> Sulch sorw I walke with
> For beste of bon and blod.[14]

Roughly translated: "Birds in the wood, the fishes in the flood, and I must go mad. Much sorrow I walk with for [and here we have either] the best of bone and blood or the beast of bone and blood." The two possible closings create a religious or erotic message ambivalently.

As early as the thirteenth-century Harley manuscript 2253 beginning "Wynter wakeneth al my care," a corresponding lyric tradition reflects upon the sleeplessness and worry of winter. William Dunbar's "A Meditation In Winter" describes the "mystie vapouris, cluddis and skyis" and says that "Nature all curage me denyis / Of sangis, ballattis and of playis."[15] Gavin Douglas's *Eneados*, his Middle Scots translation of the *Aeneid* composed from 1513 to 1525 and published in 1553, framed Virgil's epic within the progress of a year. Each of the epic's twelve books, supplemented by a translation of the thirteenth book continuation by the humanist Maphaeus Vegius, is linked to a month in a year that extends from June to June, and Douglas added a set of "nature prologues" for certain books. In his December prologue, he

POETRY'S NATURE

expresses his exhaustion and writes in end-stopped lines of the devastation of winter:

> And, thocht I wery was, me list not tyre,
> Full laith to leif our wark swa in the myre,
> Or ʒit to stynt for bitter storm or rane.
> Heir I assayt to ʒok our pleuch agane,
> And, as I couth, with afald diligens,
> This nixt buke following of profond sentens
> Has thus begun in the chil wyntir cald,
> Quhen frostis doith ourfret baith firth and fald. &c.[16]

In modern English:

> And though I was weary, I didn't like to tire / So low as to leave our work in this way in the mire / Or yet to stint because of bitter storm or rain. / Here I tried to yoke our plow again / And, so far as I could, with sincerest diligence / this next book following, in consideration, / has thus begun in the chill winter cold, / when frost adorns both wood and earth.[17]

All in all, the passage of the seasons and the life of flowers frames the measure of the poetic sequence.

In the 1930s, Rosemond Tuve wrote a pathbreaking book on the seasons in medieval poetry. There she pointedly distinguished between the general descriptions of the seasons that suffused Goliardic and troubadour verse, and what she characterized as a new concreteness in the Elizabethan uses of the theme.[18] Turning to Shakespeare's sonnets, for example, we find forty explicit mentions of the seasons—with summer outnumbering winter by two, spring by three, and autumn by seven. Yet this counting doesn't do justice to those sonnets, including Sonnet 73, that allude to

38

## THE SEASONS: PARADIGM OF LYRIC TIME

the seasons, often with some or none or few images that provide an even more refined picture of seasonal experience.

And summer appears as early as the second quatrain in Sonnet 5:

> Those hours, that with gentle work did frame
> The lovely gaze where every eye doth dwell,
> Will play the tyrants to the very same
> And that unfair which fairly doth excel;
> For never-resting time leads summer on
> To hideous winter and confounds him there,
> Sap check'd with frost and lusty leaves quite gone,
> Beauty o'er-snow'd and bareness everywhere.
> Then, were not summer's distillation left
> A liquid prisoner pent in walls of glass,
> Beauty's effect with beauty were bereft,
> Nor it nor no remembrance what it was.
>> But flowers distill'd, though they with winter meet,
>> Leese but their show; their substance still lives sweet.

The forgetting of a season when it passes is perhaps inevitable, and yet as the seasons are not known through chronology, they do appear to us, as they do within the Japanese system of fixed allusions, as signs. We see hints of their arrival as we attend to change. In the United States, of course, we have our trusted, if not often reliable, groundhog. But everywhere seasons reveal themselves subtly and then boldly and they reward our attention, much as poems do.

By Shakespeare's time the dynamic between human fertility and mortality was a poetic convention and that dynamic's analogy to artistic creation and enduring fame extended back to Horace's odes. Processes of reproduction and production had become fundamental to the very notion of the poetic series and its presentation of time. Petrarch's Rime 9, for example, famously links the role of the sun's rays in providing April's growth to the powers of Laura as she awakens with the rays of her eyes the thoughts, gestures, and words of her lover.

> Quando 'l pianeta che distingue l'ore
> ad albergar col Tauro si ritorna,
> cade vertù da l'infiammate corna
> che veste il mondo di novel colore;
>
> et non pur quel che s'apre a noi di fore,
> le rive e i colli, di fioretti adorna,
> ma dentro, dove giamai non s'aggiorna,
> gravido fa di sé il terrestro umore,
>
> onde tal frutto et simile si colga.
> Così costei, ch' è tra le donne un sole,
> in me movendo de' begli occhi i rai
>
> cria d'amor penseri atti et parole:
> ma come ch'ella gli governi o volga,
> primavera per me pur non è mai.

Here is a translation:

> When the planet that spells the hours
> returns to Taurus, virtue falling from his glowing horns
> dresses the world in fresh colors.
>
> And not only what opens before us
> the river's banks and the hills, does he fill with flowers,
> but also, in the interior, where daylight never shows itself,
> he impregnates the humid earth

## THE SEASONS: PARADIGM OF LYRIC TIME

so that it will produce fruit like this and others, too.
Therefore she who is a sun among women
sends to me the rays of her sparkling eyes

creating thoughts of love, acts and words,
but no matter how she points and turns them
my Spring still never comes.

Robert Durling notes in his edition of the poems that the sonnet seems to have accompanied a gift of truffles.[19] Petrarch derides his own aspirations of growth by vividly contrasting the warm fertility of a womb-like earth to his own state of constantly deferred conception.

Spenser similarly uses vicarious and ambivalent birth images in his *Amoretti*: "Unquiet thought, whom at the first I bred, | Of th'inward bale of my love pined hart: | and sithens have with sights and sorrowes fed, | till greater than my wombe thou woxen art."[20] And in "Astrophil and Stella," Sidney describes the commencement of the poetic sequence with the labor of childbirth, which begins not in the womb but the heart: "Thus great with child to speak, and helpless in my throes, | Biting my truant pen, beating my self for spite, | 'Fool,' said my Muse to me, 'looke in thy heart and write.'"[21]

When Shakespeare holds that "men as plants increase" in Sonnet 15 he helps us ask what kinds of growth a human being might share not only with a plant, but also with a poem.

When I consider everything that grows
Holds in perfection but a little moment,
That this huge stage presenteth nought but shows
Whereon the stars in secret influence comment;
When I perceive that men as plants increase,

POETRY'S NATURE

Cheerèd and checked even by the selfsame sky,
Vaunt in their youthful sap, at height decrease,
And wear their brave state out of memory;
Then the conceit of this inconstant stay
Sets you most rich in youth before my sight,
Where wasteful Time debateth with Decay
To change your day of youth to sullied night;
    And all at war with Time for love of you,
    As he takes from you, I engraft you new.

The dynamic of the first two quatrains is shaped by the enjamb-ment: "When I consider everything that grows" looks like a complete, if impossible, thought. And then it keeps going, shat-tering its own completion, like all growing things "holding in perfection" but a moment before we are given a set of verbs for what happened: "cheered" and "checked" letting us know growth is happening not at a measured pace, but in spurts and halts. Like a sudden thought, a burst pod, a seed dispersed, a notion recon-sidered. Human beings, when considered as single organisms, are like single plants that will "vaunt in their youthful sap and at height decrease." "Wear" indicates finery here and visual display, but also erosion. What vanishes from memory is the presence of the organism itself. At the final "then" quatrain the poem's own agency begins to emerge, the concept with which the poem began "of this inconstant stay." The stay is a prop that props the poem's argument, and the extent of that presence: the length of a life, the length of a perception, the length of a relation between persons.

Here is one of Shakespeare's innovations, for he knows that conception by seed is not the only possibility and that an old plant might generate a new one by grafting. And grafting as a

THE SEASONS: PARADIGM OF LYRIC TIME

pun on inscribing becomes the work of the poem itself, a writing, he contends, subject neither to wear or change, but carried forward by collective memory.[22] Perhaps the most well-known of the procreation sonnets, this poem gives organic growth as it is cheered and checked a temporal form, from youth to decay. And out of memory that temporal dimension would later be endowed with narrative consequences. Yet explicitly in keeping with Shakespeare's sense throughout the sequence that sonnets can animate or maintain the life of their objects, the poem might outlast even the presumed permanence of marble and other mineral forms. Immediately, in Sonnet 16, he will take a turn back to human reproduction and suggest "means more blessed than my barren rhyme," urging the young man to expend his seed, to give away in order to keep himself, to repair his life, to live.

The sonnet sequence seems to have a formal, if not natural, affinity to notions of growth, and it is not surprising that stichic forms as well provide a means for extending the individual work. Let's turn to another major poem concerned with how human beings as plants increase: William Cowper's unfinished masterpiece, "Yardley Oak."[23] For one way that seasons and years are remembered and measured is through the growth of trees and the memories held by their rings. The many allusions to leaves and flowers in the titles of poetry anthologies invite us to think of the process of reading books as analogous to the process of seeing the unfurling and blossoming of these forms, whether annual or perennial. Yet of all plant forms, trees are most likely to outlive us. So far as we know so far, their life span indicates they can live from the palm tree's fifty years to the bristlecone pine's 5,000 years.

43

"Yardley Oak" in actuality was written in the shadow of two oak trees.[24] Cowper liked to take walks to both. One was an oak in Yardley Chase near Olney that he once measured himself, leaving a memorandum in his own handwriting that it was 22 feet 6 inches in circumference. There he mentions it was said to have been planted by Judith, daughter of William the Conquerer. After his death it became known as "Cowper's oak," and apparently it was still leafing out at the turn to the nineteenth century and lasted well into the twentieth century. This is the tree that was engraved for the frontispiece to Hayley's 1806 "Supplementary Pages to the Life of Cowper" (see Figure 3). William Hayley notes there that the engraving is taken from an 1804 painting made on the spot. The second oak, sited in Yardley Lodge, was even older and larger: its girth was 28 feet 5 inches. Cowper's cousin and later biographer John Johnson notes that it was "quite in decay" and "almost hollow."[25] This state has had a clear visual influence on the poem as Cowper writes in lines 110–12:

> Embowell'd now, and of thy antient self
> Possessing nought but the scoop'd rind that seems
> An huge throat calling to the clouds for drink

The first tree's relation to Judith and the second's physical decrepitude both enter into the poem "Yardley Oak," and we could think of the poem as a third tree created in Cowper's imagination.[26]

Cowper began composing the poem at some point between his sixtieth birthday in November of 1791 and his writing of a review of Erasmus Darwin's "Economy of Vegetation" in the summer of 1792. The autograph manuscript of 184 lines was not published until 1803 when it appeared in Hayley's posthumous

## THE SEASONS: PARADIGM OF LYRIC TIME

**Figure 3** "Judith, or Cowper's Oak: A Portrait from Nature" drawn by Mrs. [Margaret] Meen, 1804, engraved by Caroline Watson, 1805, published 1806 by J. Seagrave for J. Johnson, Chichester, in William Hayley, "Supplementary pages to the Life of Cowper: containing the additions made to that work on reprinting it in octavo"

biography and collection of Cowper's writings.[27] The work is a remarkable meditation on time and history, composed, we could say, in the form of the circular time line that the tree itself offers as a model, for the poem is organized recursively as a set of reflections on time and change. The work thus does not close, but ends in a semi-colon suspended before the blank remainder of the page.

In Cowper's historical and literary imagination, the earliest references here are to the naming work of Adam in the Garden of Eden and to the sacred oaks of the Druids. Cowper views the tree as the sole survivor of an original forest and says in his opening apostrophe:

> Relicts of Ages! Could a mind imbued
> With truth from heav'n created thing adore,
> I might with rev'rence kneel and worship Thee.
>
> (lines 6–8)

He goes on to imagine the birth of the tree from the acorn, which he describes as like the child's toy of a cup and ball. And he says that he would not ask the tree to speak to him of the future, as those who visited the oracle of Dodona did, but rather to speak of the past:

> By thee I might correct, erroneous oft,
> The Clock of History, fact and events
> Timing more punctual, unrecorded facts
> Recov'ring, and mis-stated setting right.
> Desp'rate attempt till Trees shall speak again!
>
> (lines 45–9)

Although the tree has outlived its popularity and no birds roost on it now, he says it is still possible that "... verse [might] rescue thee awhile ...."

THE SEASONS: PARADIGM OF LYRIC TIME

Cowper traces all the stages of the tree's growth and decay: first seedling,

> Then twig, then saplin, and as century rolled
> Slow after century, a giant bulk
> Of girth enormous, with moss-cushion'd root
> Upheav'd above the soil, and sides imboss'd
> With prominent wens globose, till at the last
> The rottenness which Time is charged to inflict
> ... found also Thee.
>
> (lines 62–8)

He underscores the mutability of all natural forms in time: "Change is the diet on which all subsist / Created changeable, and Change at last / Destroys them" (lines 72–4). He goes on to describe how skies, heat, solar beams, clouds, storms, moisture, and drought

> Invigorate by turns the springs of life
> In all that live, plant, animal, and man,
> And in conclusion mar them. Natures threads
> ...
> Delight in agitation, yet sustain
> The force that agitates not unimpaired, ...
>
> (lines 78–83)

If we think of poems as not only occurring in time, but also as creating spans of time, the vast compass of this poem dwarfs Cowper's lived experience and places his existence in relation to human history and natural history at once. Cowper himself invites us to consider history and time as distinctly different. The final lines of his manuscript portray History, "not wanted yet," leaning on her elbow, watching Time, "whose course / Eventful should supply her with a theme" (lines 183–5).

No one knows whether Cowper had planned to extend the poem into an autobiographical meditation or some other kind of discourse. But for clues to his thinking let's look more closely for a moment at the passage from lines 144–66 that is excised from some versions:

> Thou, like myself, hast stage by stage attain'd
> Life's wintry bourn; thou, after many years,
> I after few; but few or many prove
> A span in retrospect; for I can touch
> With my least fingers' end my own decease
> And with extended thumb my natal hour,
> And hadst thou also skill in measurement
> As I, the Past would seem as short to thee.
> Evil and few—said Jacob—at an age
> Thrice mine, and few and evil, I may think,
> The Prediluvian race, whose buxom youth
> Endured two centuries, accounted theirs.
> 'Short-lived as foliage is the race of man.'
> 'The wind shakes down the leaves, the budding grove'
> 'Soon teems with others, and in spring they grow.'
> 'So pass mankind. One generation meets'
> 'Its destin'd period, and a new succeeds.'
> Such was the tender but undue complaint
> Of the Maeonian in old time; for who
> Would drawl out centuries in tedious strife,
> Severe with mental and corporeal ill,
> And would not rather chuse a shorter race
> To glory, a few decads here below?

Cowper himself provided a manuscript note explaining: "The lines mark'd with inverted commas are borrowed from my own Translation of Homer Iliad 6. Line 175." This is the famous speech of the Trojan ally Glaucus from *Iliad* Book 6, a speech that compares the generations of men to the generations of leaves. Book 6 also narrates the encounter of Hector under the great oak at the Scaen gate of Troy where the women and children await news of the war.

William Cowper was no Hector. He was a fragile man, physically and mentally—his mother had died when he was six, his father when he was thirty-five, and he had no offspring. He was to live nine years after he began this poem and he worked on his Homer translation up until 1800, the year of his death.[28] Cowper's poem returns us to the thoughts in Shakespeare's Sonnet 15, for here we find another practice of engrafting. Cowper has inserted a shoot from Homer's texts into his own and at the same time used his translation to generate new material in "Yardley Oak" itself. In this passage we see that literary history as a practice of citation merged with self-citation can be the very sustenance of the poem's growth and perhaps the poet's fame.

Let's complete this sketch of some of the relations between lyric time and the seasons by considering two brief poems by Keats, a poet also steeped in literary history who had an interest in seasonality. In March of 1818, Keats wrote this sonnet, "The Human Seasons," including it in an early draft of a letter to Benjamin Bailey:

> Four seasons fill the measure of the year;
>> There are four seasons in the mind of man.
> He has his lusty Spring, when fancy clear
>> Takes in all beauty with an easy span.
> He has his Summer, when luxuriously
>> Spring's honeyed cud of youthful thought he loves
> To ruminate, and by such dreaming nigh

POETRY'S NATURE

His nearest unto heaven. Quiet coves
His soul has in its Autumn, when his wings
    He furleth close; contented so to look
On mists in idleness—to let fair things
    Pass by unheeded as a threshold brook.
He has his Winter too of pale misfeature,
Or else he would forego his mortal nature.[29]

The poem does not break much new ground with regard to the qualities of the seasons, but its allegory is concerned with the progression of the seasons and the analogy between the span of a year and the span of a life. The concluding thoughts on mortality in winter are resonant to these lines in *Endymion*, which he wrote in the same period:

O may no wintry season, bare and hoary,
See it half finished; but let Autumn bold,
With universal tinge of sober gold,
Be all about me when I make an end.[30]

In these lines Keats is setting out the rather astonishing timetable, which he actually met, for finishing his long poem. Yet there is an echo here of the fact that each year we each pass a date we don't know and can't know: our own death date. Keats had a kind of season of concern with the seasons in those months. In December, finished with the exhausting labor of finishing *Endymion*, he took a few days of extended rest at the Fox and Hounds Inn in Burford Bridge, Surrey. He had arrived at the wintry season he dreaded and wrote a brief lyric poem about it. Keats did not provide a title for this lyric, and he never referred to it in his letters. Known sometimes as "Song," and sometimes "Stanzas," and sometimes simply "Poem," it is now most often

## THE SEASONS: PARADIGM OF LYRIC TIME

anthologized with its first line as the title "In drear-nighted December."

> In drear-nighted December,
>    Too happy, happy tree,
> Thy branches ne'er remember
>    Their green felicity:
> The north cannot undo them,
> With a sleety whistle through them,
> Nor frozen thawings glue them
>    From budding at the prime.
>
> In drear-nighted December,
>    Too happy, happy brook,
> Thy bubblings ne'er remember
>    Apollo's summer look;
> But with a sweet forgetting,
> They stay their crystal fretting,
> Never, never petting
>    About the frozen time.
>
> Ah! would 'twere so with many
>    A gentle girl and boy!
> But were there ever any
>    Writh'd not [at] passèd joy?
> The feel of not to feel it,
> When there is none to heal it
> Nor numbèd sense to steel it,
>    Was never said in rhyme.[31]

It is often noted that the poem is in a form Keats took from Dryden. In fact Dryden, as far as I can tell, used this form only once, but memorably so: in the tripping bittersweet reflections on love in the song "Farewell ungrateful traitor" from "The Spanish

Fryar." Queen Leonora, suffering an ostensible rejection by her husband, asks her maid Teresa to sing it, saying "Sing me the Song which poor Olympia made / when false Bireno left her." Therefore as Keats is echoing Dryden, Dryden is echoing Ariosto.[32]

Keats here has something to say about natural history and human history, memory and forgetting, and feeling and the inability to feel. Keats had to forget *Endymion*, a project he'd been obsessed with for months, in order to write it. Keats had to remember, perhaps voluntarily, perhaps involuntarily, the plaint of Dryden's Leonora, who had to remember the plaint of Ariosto's Olympia (and we could keep going, since Olympia is in turn echoing the plaint of Ariadne abandoned by Theseus).

Let's look, too, at the poem's references to time: *night*; *December*; *prime*; *summer*; *frozen time*.

Considering this list, we might ask: how often do things happen? Night, months, ritual hours and clock time, seasons, natural processes, and the flow of experience into the past are always the case. But what happens in cycles, to be known as cycles, must be noted in perception. The patterns of nature are undergone by all species, yet human viewers discern such patterns as patterns. And patterns that can be noticed as patterns also can mark absences or be characterized by absence. Here, within a framework of always, we also have a series of nevers: "never remember green felicity"; "never remember Apollo's summer look"; "never never petting"; and, significantly, "never said in rhyme."

Human beings have the capacity to note what is not present as well as what is and the imagination to give what is not present a name or form. Keats would work on the power of making out of negation most famously in the negative capability letter he wrote in this same December period. And the words of "In

# THE SEASONS: PARADIGM OF LYRIC TIME

drear-nighted December" would echo through his later poems. The "happy, happy dove" of the "Ode to Psyche" most probably came first. Then the "Ode on a Grecian Urn"'s "happy, happy boughs! that cannot shed / Your leaves, nor ever bid the Spring adieu," its "happy melodist" and "More happy love! more happy, happy love!" And the "Ode to a Nightingale"'s bird "too happy" in its happiness.[33] The "too happy happy" tree and brook of "In drear-nighted December" are shaped by destinies that seem to be numb to suffering: the process of their growth and continuance accommodates changes in the environment that would seem to be unbearable.

Where does their power of resistance find its source? In their "sweet forgetting," their inability to remember, their resistance to feeling. We might say, following the argument Keats is setting out, this power of staying stems from their inability to find significance or to organize their experiences around the singular fate of their being. To know a change and feel it represents the human perspective, the perspective of those who remember the past. The feel of not to feel it, however, returns us to what we assume but can't really know is the insensible hibernation of the natural world. This feeling of trees and brooks that do not need healing or steeling is not said in human rhyme because we do not know it. It is unlike us, as unlike us as the noumenal is unlike the phenomenal.

I will mention in closing a few other aspects of the work. Metonymy rules through the imagery here. Keats explores the bound relation between the processes of freezing and thawing, a fundamentally metonymic connection; the state of the part speaks for the being of the whole. It is the branches that are the tree, the branches that will bud, the bubblings that are the brook, those crystallized bubblings that will melt. A number of individual words Keats has chosen have the quality of primal words and so themselves have the quality of two states: *writhe*—to make a wreath and also to twist in agony (in eighteenth-century Scotland a writhe of snow was a snowbank); *fret*—to erode, decay, but also to make an ornamental pattern; *petting*—to pout but also to be cosseted; *to stay*—to remain in place and to resist or arrest. And, above all, *happy* itself—for happiness that is too happy, the kind we find in trees and doves and nightingales, seems a happiness derived from *hap* or chance. All chances are happy, but a happy chance incorporates the risk of chance and the certainty of a feeling of fulfillment. The connotative atmosphere around these words is one of binding, and we remember these lines from the opening of *Endymion*:

> Therefore, on every morrow, are we wreathing
> A flowery band to bind us to the earth,
> Spite of despondence, of the inhuman dearth
> Of noble natures, of the gloomy days,
> Of all the unhealthy and o'er-darkened ways
> Made for our searching: yes, in spite of all,
> Some shape of beauty moves away the pall
> From our dark spirits.[34]

"When there is none to heal it" in 1817 brings to mind Keats's brother Tom and his suffering from tuberculosis. Keats's feel of not to feel it carries forward the transformative power of feeling and healing against the temporality of pain. Does time heal or simply bring more agony?

Nature is not animal here: the numbed sense is the stoicism of nonanimal nature and the certainty of happy love reveals itself as love beneath the rule of chance. The poem also underscores the

## THE SEASONS: PARADIGM OF LYRIC TIME

capacity of human beings to suffer not only in the present when pain must be endured, but as well out of memories of the past, including memories that come to us of the lives of others through poems.

In the end, what *is* said in rhyme? As Coleridge taught us before Keats, rhyme is both a crystal fretting, a substance dependent upon the initial matter that forms it, and an echoing sound undergoing constant transformation. We know that change and feel it.

# III

# MOTION AND TURN: WATER'S WAYS

Emerging in time, poems are in motion. When a poem also takes on the representation of motion the effect is like the familiar experience of coming into a station beside another train on a parallel track: are we moving? or is the other train moving? or are we both moving? The sensation depends upon both trains, but we could never say it is reciprocal, never a matter of turn-taking—it is an effect of perception by an observer who, too, is moving and being moved.

Let's take a look at two poems of animal motion, both dating to the 1930s and both by now well-known works of Modernism. The first I would cite is e. e. cummings's anagrammatic poem on a grasshopper, "r-p-o-p-h-e-s-s-a-g-r." cummings joins a long line of poets noting the joy and ephemerality of grasshopper existence in a tradition that ranges at least from Anacreon to Richard Lovelace. cummings's poem could be read aloud, yet there is no convention available for reading it aloud. We're on our own. We could say that the poem silences us. Or that the

*Poetry's Nature*. Susan Stewart, Oxford University Press. © Susan Stewart (2025).
DOI: 10.1093/9780192577689.003.0003

POETRY'S NATURE

poem passes its originality on to us. In either case, let's look at it silently for a moment:

<pre>
                              r-p-o-p-h-e-s-s-a-g-r
                    who
        a)s w(e loo)k
        upnowgath
                    PPEGORHRASS
                              eringint(o-
        aThe):l
              eA
                 !p:
        S                                   a
                    (r
        rIvInG              .gRrEaPsPhOs)
                                        to
        rea(be)rran(com)gi(e)ngly
        ,grasshopper;[1]
</pre>

There, at its center is a leap—we can see it, but we can't meet it.

The second poem is William Carlos Williams's "Poem":

As the cat
climbed over
the top of

the jamcloset
first the right
forefoot

carefully
then the hind
stepped down

into the pit of
the empty
flowerpot[2]

58

## MOTION AND TURN: WATER'S WAYS

Part of the brilliance of Williams's poem is that he has taken enjambment—a feature of lines that usually makes us tumble forward—and made us inch along a series of precipices. He has slowed down the dimeter, and separated the adjectives from their nouns and stranded the sole adverb, "carefully," far from either possible verb. cummings's poem, with its kairotic emphasis upon the moment of the leap no doubt owes a great deal to photography, as Williams's slow-motion depiction of the descent of the cat owes a great deal to cinema. Both poems, eschewing any tensions between rhythm and meter, zero in on pictorial effects, the first a glimpse, the second a motion picture.

Yet if we look at the representation of motion in earlier texts that draw on conventions of metrical verse, we find a broad array of means for transferring the motion of the poem to the motion represented and on to the moving eye and thoughts of the reader/speaker. These transferences, which we might think of as shared vibrations and pulses, lend emotional power to the work as they also effect the more general carrying over into meaning that we associate with the turns of tropes, metaphors, and metonymy. Consider, in this regard, a poem registering motion and its absence—Wordsworth's "A slumber did my spirit seal":

A slumber did my spirit seal;
   I had no human fears:
She seemed a thing that could not feel
   The touch of earthly years.

No motion has she now, no force;
   She neither hears nor sees,
Rolled round in earth's diurnal course
   With rocks and stones and trees.[3]

# POETRY'S NATURE

This poem brings feeling very close to what, as we saw in my second lecture, Keats would call "the feel of not to feel it"—the feeling of coming up against numbed sense or the absence of feeling. Wordsworth's eight lines also bring what was thought of in his time as the inorganic very close to the organic. Perhaps because of this valence between the felt and the numb, which extends here to the relation between the sentient and the nonsentient, the living and the dead, the animate and the inanimate, the usual questions we bring to a poem, "Who is talking? And who is listening?" are especially hard to answer. We can look to the poem's specific historical context and ask, as many others have before us—who was Lucy? What was her fate? We can wonder what the poem's attitudes toward the inanimate tell us about Wordsworth's fear of death, his loneliness as he wrote this and the other poems we know as the Lucy poems during his sojourn in Germany or his interest in the near-death experiences of trance states that in this period intrigued him, his sister Dorothy, and Coleridge.[4]

The speaker switches from first-person expression in the first two lines ["A slumber did *my* spirit seal; I had no human fears"] to description in the third person in the next two ["She *seemed* a thing that could not feel"]. In the second, concluding stanza, in the third person, the speaker reports an absence of feeling. But on closer look, it is literally difficult to countenance that point of view—the speaker notes something missing: she has no motion or force. The speaker then takes the point of view that can only be held by the "she"—she neither hears nor sees. This inference can be made on the basis of the "she" being rolled round in earth's diurnal course like other inanimate or nonhuman forms—rocks, and stones, and trees. There is something off balance about the scale of this small list: not only the horror of a human being rolled about like a mere thing, but also the near redundancy of rocks and stones, which can be loosened from the earth, and trees which cannot be unearthed and remain trees.

The more we consider this poem, the stranger it becomes as a set of statements. When would the speaker find his or her spirit sealed and an absence of human fears? Presumably when dead. Is to seem a thing to be a thing? The seeming is all in the eye of the beholder and not the "she." What is "she" if she is stripped of agency and sense impression, passively enduring natural forces possibly known only through those senses not mentioned—feeling or touch? Presumably she is dead.

And what of the time frame of the poem? Is this a temporary or eternal slumber? How does the touch of earthly years measure against the earth's daily rotation on the one hand and against eternity on the other? Do the dead live in days rather than years or immeasurable spans of time? And what is the trajectory of the diurnal course? Rocks and stones and trees may be rolled round daily, but they are long-lived forms, as we've just considered.

To grasp the long duration, the almost Sisyphean cast of Wordsworth's final image, we can think of the direct contrast to it offered by a poem like Richard Crashaw's "Bulla" or Bubble. Crashaw's Latin poem is 157 lines long, but seems to unspool in an instant. Comparing the formation of the bubble to the emergence of Venus from the sea, he speeds through impressions of color, pattern, motion, and light, saying, in George Walton Williams's translation:

> I am the brief nature of the
> wind. To be sure, I am the flower of air,
> the star of the sea, as it were,
> the golden wit of nature,

the rambling tale of nature,
the brief dream of nature ...
distinguished by snows, roses,
waves, fires, air
painted, bejewelled, and golden,
O I am, of course, O nothing.

The final lines bear a final surprise:

If it is painful and long lasting to have drawn out this
    pomposity into boredom
    and my Bubble seems too old;
Lift your eyes and this light trifle will fly away.
    A Fate, not busy with her agile hand, will cut it off.
Still it lived. Why did it live? Indeed [because] you
    read this far.
Indeed it was time then to have been able to die.[5]

A similarly fleeting effervescence can be found in the chorus of Shelley's "Hellas":

Worlds on worlds are rolling ever
    From creation to decay,
Like the bubbles on a river
    Sparkling, bursting, borne away ...[6]

In Crashaw and Shelley, natural motion surrounds us with signs of life's presence even as particulars vanish. In contrast, Wordsworth's imagery is indicative of a leaden and tragic realization: the speaker is worlds away from the "she."

Here such devices as prosopopoeia and personification can be viewed as more than strategies of animation. Such figures are examples of what the anthropologist Carlo Severi has called

## MOTION AND TURN: WATER'S WAYS

"chimeric objects"—those that express the relation between a manifested form and a mentally projected form.[7] Wordsworth himself comes close to this idea when he claims that "objects derive their influence not from properties inherent in them but from such as are bestowed upon them by the minds of those who are conversant with or affected by these objects."[8] After Wordsworth, John Ruskin both named and condemned the pathetic fallacy, arguing that saying the natural world has human feelings is so irrational it borders between a kind of madness and "prophetic inspiration."[9] Nevertheless, even if the clouds do not weep for us, we might imagine they do. It does not rain in our hearts as it rains in the town, but we might feel that it does. These projections come quite close as well to Eliot's notion of the "objective correlative," where the inward mode recognizes itself in a projected object of perception.[10]

Beyond the restrained emotions expressed in "A slumber did my spirit seal," Wordsworth also seems to have taken on some of the formal problems involved in representing motion in an art form that is itself inherently both moving and alive. Here the end-stopped lines that begin each stanza turn to enjambment in each stanza's concluding lines. It is as if something is being held off and then released, held off and released—it is difficult to write a dead, a numb, poem at least in part because motion in time is intrinsic to the speaking voice. Along with the extraocular muscles of the eye, the laryngeal muscles are the fastest-firing muscles in our bodies, three to five times faster than we can run. Even when we are reading silently, the larynx responds with small subvocalizing movements to reproduce the sounds of the words we are following visually.[11]

With all its efforts toward stilling human action before the sublime scale shift to the indiscernible movements of the earth's diurnal course, Wordsworth's poem could be considered one of the most paradigmatic examples of an attempt to create a poem as "nature mort" or, as we say in English, still life. For centuries it has been part of visual art pedagogy to train draughtsmen and painters by means of representing still objects under various conditions of light, shadow, and composition. Nevertheless, it seems to be impossible to write "the feel of not to feel it" in poetry—we remember that feeling "was never said in rhyme."

Freezing and motion and bubbles necessarily bring us to what is perhaps the quintessential image of motion in poetry and other art forms, and that is the flow of water. As Heraclitus famously noted,[12] the perception of flowing water is a primal human experience of the fleetingness of perception itself and water has become the central metaphor of so many poems concerned with perceptual limits and possibilities. Such poems return us to the juxtaposition of the immediate, lived, life of change and the desire for immortality or permanence so characteristic of Renaissance sonnet sequences. Indeed, from Wordsworth's River Duddon sonnets to the picaresque ethnography of Alice Oswald's *Dart*, some of the most enduring English poetry concerned with streams and rivers has a common structure. Such poems rely upon the shifting and paradoxical relationship between a poet moving sequentially in time and the evident permanence of named places and persons encountered along the way.

Today, under these general considerations of the representation of motion, I would like to take up a set of poems that all are concerned with not only the movement of water, but also

## MOTION AND TURN: WATER'S WAYS

the forms posed by water. These are poems that bring forward an aspect of poetic practice that has to do with motion in sense impression and in thought; that is, the relation of sense impression to causal inference and the felt dimension of pattern that we know through rhythm. My focus will be poems concerned with the connections between the representation of motion in the world and the work of metonymy and other tropes in the service of such representations. Turns, burdens, carrying-over, transformations, tenors, and vehicles—the language of tropes is the language of transport, not only the carrying over or extension of phenomena into meaning, but as well the carrying over of meaning to emotion and insight.

Let's begin by looking at Henry Vaughan's mid-seventeenth-century poem "The Water-fall" with its patterns of slowing and spilling forth. Like all shape poems, "The Water-fall" reveals its visual form through the unfolding of its lines in time. Yet Vaughan's is an unusual shape poem in that in the end it depicts and imitates not a bounded visual form, but the process of a waterfall and the ongoing sequences of transformation that characterize it and eventually its beholder. It may be useful to remember what an actual waterfall is, for Vaughan and for us:

> any point in a river or stream where water flows over a vertical drop or a series of steep drops. They are most commonly formed when a river courses over a top layer of resistant bedrock before falling on to softer rock. The softer rock erodes at a faster rate than the bedrock, leading to an increasingly high drop of water, which plunges into a pool and often a successive stream or streams.

A waterfall, while always in process as a form, is also a location in a given range of space. It has a particular import for its local species of birds and insects and the human beings who dwell near a waterfall often will give it a name.[13]

It is worth pausing further on this tension between process and form. For the philosopher of science and former naval officer Michel Serres, arguing for the contributions of the atomists to our intuitions of form, a waterfall is the foundation or origin of the dynamic between flow and reversal that comes to characterize all experiences of rhythm. He writes: "In the beginning is the cataract, the waterfall: here is the *rhein*, the rhesis"—that is, the flow of fresh water. But it is the *dinos* or vortex that follows that sparks "a momentary reversibility" to the irreversibility of the flow: the result is *rhuthmos* or the phenomenon of rhythm. More recent philosophers of ontology have argued that the waterfall epitomizes the tension between object and process: "the water falls, but the waterfall does not fall."[14] The waterfall is a self-shaping, self-forming process of transformation. A paradigm for rhythm, it is thereby a form and process at once and particularly suited to kairotic poems of transformed and transforming insight. As the poet Jay Wright recently has written in his meditation, "An Examination of Rhythm," "rhythm, however we conceive it, appears as a malleable form that establishes a new identity or speaks to an identity in shape-shifting."[15]

Even if Henry Vaughan did not give his waterfall a name, let's pay attention to the rhythm of its particular flows and vortices:

> With what deep murmurs through time's silent stealth
> Doth thy transparent, cool, and watery wealth
> > Here flowing fall,
> > And chide, and call,

## MOTION AND TURN: WATER'S WAYS

As if his liquid, loose retinue stayed
Ling'ring, and were of this steep place afraid,
    The common pass
    Where, clear as glass,
    All must descend
    Not to an end,
But quickened by this deep and rocky grave,
Rise to a longer course more bright and brave.
Dear stream! dear bank, where often I
Have sat, and pleased my pensive eye,
Why, since each drop of thy quick store
Runs thither, whence it flowed before,
Should poor souls fear a shade or night,
Who came (sure) from a sea of light?
Or since those drops are all sent back
So sure to thee, that none doth lack,
Why should frail flesh doubt any more
That what God takes, he'll not restore?
O useful element and clear!
My sacred wash and cleanser here,
My first consigner unto those
Fountains of life, where the Lamb goes?
What sublime truths, and wholesome themes,
Lodge in thy mystical, deep streams!
Such as dull man can never find
Unless that Spirit lead his mind,
Which first upon thy face did move,
And hatched all with his quickening love.
As this loud brook's incessant fall
In streaming rings restagnates all,
Which reach by course the bank, and then
Are no more seen, just so pass men.
O my invisible estate,
My glorious liberty, still late!

> Thou art the channel my soul seeks,
> Not this with cataracts and creeks.[16]

In the opening to the poem, Vaughan vividly gives a sense of how a waterfall is heard before it is seen. He literally amplifies the sound from deep murmurs to the chiding and calling of the moment of the drop to the quickening final course. It is truly one of the fastest and most precipitous openings of English poems and this sense of quickness is effected not only by the sound imagery, but as well by the resonance of the couplet rhymes popping up as he moves from a pentameter pair to a dimeter pair, back to pentameter, then an intensification, doubling, of the dimeter couplets to the resolved final pentameter. In fact, dimeter, in two-beat lines or doubled as song meter, from the tumbling lyrics of John Skelton to the joyful outbursts of Wordsworth's Intimations Ode, often indicates singing or speech play, especially when it is juxtaposed to the spoken quality of pentameter lines.

The endearment Vaughan extends to his interlocutor, the waterfall, reminds us that this is an ode and that he has been talking to the waterfall itself: but at this point in the poem what constitutes the waterfall? The stream, the drops of water, the pool, the bank from which a human being can encounter it? Vaughan tells us that each drop is part of the circular process by which water passes between the sky and the earth. He reminds his reader that all of creation came from the sea of light recounted in Genesis 1:2: "And the earth was without form, and void; and darkness *was* upon the face of the deep. And the Spirit of God moved upon the face of the waters."

The circular processes of water are mentioned as well in Ecclesiastes 1:7, where we read: "All the rivers run into the sea; yet the sea *is* not full; unto the place from whence the rivers come, thither they return again." Such a cyclical path of water had been described as well by Plato in the *Critias*, Aristotle in his *Meteorology*, Pliny in his *Natural History*, and Seneca in his *Quaestiones Naturales*. Into the Middle Ages it was widely believed that water circulated within the earth through underground passages that purged sea water of its salinity. It was not until Bernard Palissy's *Discours Admirable* of 1580 that anyone came to understand that rainfall was enough to create and maintain rivers.[17]

We can read in Joseph Hall's discourse "Upon the Rain and the Waters" in his *The Arte of Divine Meditation* of 1606 how vapors rise from the sea to meet in a cloud, drops fall from the cloud, then run together and in rills of water meet in channels, channels run to brooks, brooks to rivers, rivers to the sea. So it is, he says, with spiritual gifts. He implores God to take the drops rained upon his soul and return them to what he calls the great ocean of glory of God's own bounty.[18] The waterfall thus is a moment of intensity in a process of circulation and here it offers a hieroglyph whose significance moves from creation to the theology of salvation.

In his next strophes Vaughan turns via metaphor to the level of the purely symbolic: the "sublime truths" and "wholesome themes" the waterfall evokes. The "useful element" of water is the water of baptism, the fountains of life; the mystical deep streams are sprung from the original creative act of God. *Restagnates* indicates not so much our contemporary meaning of putridity, as a return to calm and stillness. As human beings vanish beneath the surface in death, they are lifted up. Here symbolism is made explicit in a simile: men seem to disappear from life like the incessantly expanding rings on the surface of the pool as the water plunges there, forming a "grave" at its foot.[19] But for Vaughan these persons are actually passing into an "invisible estate"—the future life which is the smooth, "more bright and brave" channel of the life after death.

> O my invisible estate,
> My glorious liberty, still late!
> Thou art the channel my soul seeks,
> Not this with cataracts and creeks.

The poem ends with a metaphorical transposition of the concept of a channel—a word that has an array of meanings that includes, among many others, a rivulet, an artificial strait or pipe, and any line of action that might be pursued. Vaughan carries over the physical phenomenon to the metaphysical belief. His "not this" might seem at first glance a negation, but the reader is left in the end with the consonance of "cataracts and creeks"—a pair of terms that on a smaller scale enacts the sequence of the waterfall from cataract to creek. "Invisible estates" and "glorious liberty" leave us in an abstract state of seeking—it is the waterfall that gives us sounds and images to which we can attach our thoughts.

As in so much of Vaughan's poetry it is the actual and encountered natural world that has become the vehicle of a transport to the sacred and symbolic.[20] In his work, violets thriving at their roots, the dear secret greenness hidden in seeds, the new leaves and new branches of tinder, the possibility of verse itself becoming wild as weeds, and, above all, the pull of magnetism and the glinting trembling light of fire are not instances of existing concepts alone, but sparks for acknowledging the relations between things, the motion of things, and the capacity of things to move us. Praising change and mutability, Vaughan wrote in his poem "Affliction (I)": "Beauty consists in colours; and that's best / Which is not fixed, but flies, and flows."[21]

Vaughan's depictions of the world are in these ways efforts to enter into the transformations of things in time. Observing across contexts, he notes the connections between living things as much as the things in themselves. Perception, emotion, and conceptual experience go beyond the immediacy of substance; in the waterfall, as here, it is quickness and quickening—the speed of the water, the speed of the words, the sense of something coming to life like the infant in the womb—this is the matrix of animation and resurrection that shapes the form of the poem.

Let's briefly review some of the philosophy of motion at work behind Vaughan's thinking and the role of those philosophies in later thought, for as Aristotle famously wrote in his *Physics*, "if we do not know what motion is, neither do we understand what nature is."[22] Because motion is not logically or ontologically self-sufficient, it requires an explanation and Aristotle contended that every motion begins in another motion and that only living, animate organisms possess an inherent power to move. From this beginning, motion was not merely a matter of mechanics, but a phenomenon that drew on fundamental problems in ontology, philosophy, and theology. For scholastic thinkers of the twelfth and thirteenth centuries, including Peter Lombard and the discontented scholastic William of Ockham, an important dimension of the puzzle of motion included the question of whether motion was an evolving process, as Aristotle had indicated, where the terminus of the motion is the completion or perfection of the process. Yet it also became clear that an emphasis on the end point of motion draws our attention away from the very movement that is the essence of the phenomenon. There was also the question of the varying intensity and velocity of motion—not only with regard to motion in nature, but also in light of theological questions, such as the intensification and diminishment of *caritas* or the holy spirit.[23]

By the seventeenth century, Henry Vaughan's twin brother Thomas and his fellow hermeticists proposed that each creature contained a portion of a universal world spirit or soul, giving it life and force. Thomas's antagonist Henry More and his fellow Cambridge Platonists rejected the hermeticist emphasis on magic, but continued to maintain that material explanations of physical phenomena were activated by divine, incorporeal interventions at work everywhere in the universe.[24] In contrast, Galileo, Descartes, and Newton variously focused upon material questions of whether motion passed from one body to another or involved the transfer of matter in one body's context into the context of the matter of another body. By the early eighteenth century, Leibniz and Berkeley had rejected ideas of absolute motion, holding there is only relative motion and by the twentieth century most thinkers agreed.[25]

Motion remains the crux of the process under which we conceive of objects both changing and remaining the same. An object changes by assuming a different position relative to other objects and it remains the same by preserving its identity, all that is included within its reality. The problem of motion reveals the impossibility of knowing things in themselves. And each of these aspects of motion both brings forward and defers the question of cause. Whitehead can be a help again here. He wrote in his book *Modes of Thought*, "How can one event be the cause of another? The whole antecedent world conspires to produce a new occasion. But some one occasion in an important way conditions the formation of a successor. How can we understand this process of conditioning? The mere notion of transferring

MOTION AND TURN: WATER'S WAYS

a quality is entirely unintelligible." As a result, Whitehead held that a doctrine of immanence is at work in causation: the qualitative energies of the past are combined into a pattern of qualitative energies in each present occasion. Causation happens at a moment, in a place, and according to such qualities. He holds that this is one of the reasons that we feel we are involved in the world. When we observe, we observe the connectivity of the world and this enables the transmission of its types of pattern, including the laws of nature. Physical science, he contended, considers nature as activity alone—what he called "bare activity," but only through conceptual experience can content be added to such bare motion. Conceptual experience, emotion, and imagination as the consideration of alternatives, go beyond the immediacy of presentation and invite us to draw connections and find likenesses.[26]

This line of reasoning about motion and causality underscores the relation between motion and thought. Rather than conceptualizing thought as something added to physical processes, we might instead follow Hans Jonas, Susanne Langer,[27] and Whitehead himself in considering the ways that perceiving subjects are affected by the physical forces at work in the appearance of motion. Jonas discusses at length the problem that Kant and Hume generated when they separated causality from the senses. They held that causality seemed to be something added to perceptions that were given, or purely states of reception. But if this is true then we would have to deny the causality of sense perception itself and as well hold that we have no direct, experiential knowledge of force and influence.

Like wind and weather, force and influence may not be so readily visible and objectively grasped, but they are felt. Jonas concluded that "concepts of force and cause spring from a type of experience which involves 'impressions of reflection' in addition to those of 'sensation'; i.e., they involve the subject's awareness of his [or her] own inward mode of affectedness (such as the proprioceptive awareness of muscular effort) as an integral part-content of the object-experience itself."[28] Yet Jonas takes a crucial further step in saying that there is what could be called a subjective correlative in the choice of object; the projection will always involve the inference of analogous processes from the experience of perceptual immediacy, including the immediacy of felt emotion.

We can, like Descartes, try to detach the world from thought, but that leaves us with no way to explain the pressure of the world upon our lived experience or, since we are living beings in a world of living beings, the impact of forms of life upon other forms of life. Furthermore, we can try to suspend teleology, but since motion is relative, cause will always evoke prior causes and subsequent consequences. Ultimately, given the limits of the observable universe, all causal questions lead to questions of first cause. Of course, for Henry Vaughan this is not a crux, for he can find scriptural analogues for those phenomena he observes and he is confident in his paradigm for creation. The deferment of cause is part of his worldview as well as his theology, just as the political circumstances of his life made retirement and withdrawal appealing and the hermetic philosophy that surrounded him gave the hidden and the immanent great value. But for a poet who is an atheist, like Percy Shelley, causality is more problematic.

I've asked you to consider Shelley's great lyric meditation, "Mont Blanc," in advance of our meeting, for it is a poem deeply concerned with these issues. The poem's time frame is 1816: the year without a summer. The 1815 volcanic explosion of Mount Tambora in Indonesia had thrown small particles into the stratosphere that by the next summer had lowered the world's temperature by 3 degrees Celsius, destroying crops, and sending snow to New England. Percy and Mary Shelley, accompanied by Byron and other friends, were living by Lake Geneva in those months. They were kept inside most days by rain and darkness. But at the end of July Percy and Mary decided to visit the valley of Chamonix at the head of the River Arve. Percy was to write that he "never knew what mountains were before" and describes how he experienced "a sentiment of exstatic wonder, not unallied to madness," on encountering the Alps at close range.[29]

In the poem, he is standing on a bridge over the Arve; he sees the flow of the river and its valley; he hears the streams that feed it from the Mer de Glace, above, and he projects in his imagination the absent source and cause of so much force and motion. Permanence is embodied by the mountain itself, impermanence and the transitory are embodied by the river, and mediating the relation between them are the streams melting from the glacier and the myriad waterfalls that result. Shelley, like Vaughan, alludes to how these waters are part of a circular process: precipitation from invisible and inaudible lightning storms high in the mountain send down the water that will travel the Arve and later the Rhone, and evaporation from all these waters will contribute to the formation of storms above. For Shelley all these moving natural forms are embodiments or manifestations of a hidden force.

The poem is sketched as a loose Pindaric ode in five parts, appropriately made of blank verse although end-word repetition, occasional rhyme, and frequent enjambment keep the lines

POETRY'S NATURE

tumbling forward. Shelley builds a matrix of images by juxtaposing unmoving rock to moving streams of water and going on to suggest the fleeting presence of the invisible wind and effects of light and vapor: clouds and sunbeams; flames of lightning; rainbows; shadows; smoke; snow-flakes, and mists. The *vale* of Chamonix is obsessively cast as a *veil*. These transitory effects awaken his imagination to thoughts of ghosts and to worlds he conjectures might be revealed in sleep and death.

Below and beyond the bridge is the ravine that Shelley uses as an analogue for his mind and its powers. In an echo of his experience of an ecstasy there akin to madness, he plays throughout on the transposed letters of the words Arve, rave, and ravine. In Shelley's thought from this period Power with a capital P is the ever-present engine of both the forms and motions of the natural world and the forms and motions of the human mind. Shelley suggests here that Power is an unmoved mover or first cause of the universe. Its source, like the source of the Arve, is secret and the poem claims from the very beginning that the source of human thought lies in such a secret spring; the image is repeated in the last section as a secret strength.

> Dizzy Ravine! and when I gaze on thee
> I seem as in a trance sublime and strange
> To muse on my own separate phantasy,
> My own, my human mind, which passively
> Now renders and receives fast influencings,
>
> (lines 34–8)

Shelley has composed a poem that recreates the pace of his mind succumbing to the pace of the surrounding environment. Yet he is not making an imitation; ever a Platonist, Shelley is searching for abstractions and a deep form of poetic justice. The end of section III, for example, celebrates the unintelligibility of the wilderness as a source of awe, doubt, and reconciliation with nature. The mountain delivers truth to those members of the ranks of the wise, great, and good prepared to interpret and, crucially, to feel it.

> The wilderness has a mysterious tongue
> Which teaches awful doubt, or faith so mild,
> So solemn, so serene, that man may be
> But for such faith with nature reconciled;
> Thou hast a voice, great Mountain, to repeal
> Large codes of fraud and woe; not understood
> By all, but which the wise, and great, and good
> Interpret, or make felt, or deeply feel.
>
> (lines 76–83)

The conclusion of the poem, section V, returns to this claim regarding interpretation and feeling. As in so much of the poem, Shelley seems to be addressing the mountain and its surroundings, yet also clearly is talking to himself:

> Mont Blanc yet gleams on high:—the power is there,
> The still and solemn power of many sights,
> And many sounds, and much of life and death.
> In the calm darkness of the moonless nights,
> In the lone glare of day, the snows descend
> Upon that Mountain; none beholds them there,
> Nor when the flakes burn in the sinking sun,
> Or the star-beams dart through them:—Winds contend
> Silently there, and heap the snow with breath
> Rapid and strong, but silently! Its home

POETRY'S NATURE

The voiceless lightning in these solitudes
Keeps innocently, and like vapour broods
Over the snow.

(lines 127–39)

And he draws his conclusion:

The secret strength of things
Which governs thought, and to the infinite dome
Of heaven is as a law, inhabits thee!
And what were thou, and earth, and stars, and sea,
If to the human mind's imaginings
Silence and solitude were vacancy?

(lines 139–44)

The secret strength of the mountain governs thought and from the perspective of transcendence, is as a law. Yet for Shelley all such phenomena, not only the mountain—but all the earth, the stars, and the sea, are supplied with meaning through the human mind's imaginings.

Mont Blanc's glaciers were melting and changing that July day in 1816. Shelley noted this motion with dread and excitement, for he saw in the relentless progress of the glacier toward Chamonix and the shattered pines and destruction such progress caused, evidence of Buffon's theory of nature's inevitable self-devouring and entropy. Shelley wrote of the aesthetic experience of forms of nature: "*why* do they enchant … it cannot be innate, is it acquired?," continuing, "It does not prove the non-existence of a thing that it is not discoverable by reason. *Feeling* here affords us sufficient proof. I pity those who have not this demonstration," he says, "tho' I can scarce believe that such [people] exist."[30]

Let's look at one more example of a poem concerned with powers of flowing, moving water: Gerard Manley Hopkins's poem on

## MOTION AND TURN: WATER'S WAYS

the waterfall at Inversnaid on the edge of Loch Lomond. Hopkins visited the small settlement there in September 1881 and used the place name as his title. Recollecting this visit six years later in a letter on September 7, 1887, to W. M. Baillie, he wrote: "I hurried from Glasgow one day to Loch Lomond. The day was dark and partly hid the lake, yet it did not altogether disfigure it but gave a pensive or solemn beauty which left a deep impression on me."[31] In Scots Gaelic the place name means "needle confluence" or "the mouth of the needle stream." (Can we totally ignore the implicit pun in English, however, that we are one letter away from having a naiad in verse?) Here is the poem.

> This dárksome búrn, hórseback brówn,
> His rollrock highroad roaring down,
> In coop and in comb the fleece of his foam
> Flutes and low to the lake falls home.

> A windpuff-bónnet of fáwn-fróth
> Turns and twindles over the broth
> Of a póol so pítchblack, féll-frówning,
> It rounds and rounds Despair to drowning.

> Degged with dew, dappled with dew
> Are the groins of the braes that the brook treads
>     through,
> Wiry heathpacks, flitches of fern,
> And the beadbonny ash that sits over the burn.

> What would the world be, once bereft
> Of wet and of wildness? Let them be left,
> O let them be left, wildness and wet;
> Long live the weeds and the wilderness yet.

POETRY'S NATURE

Here, as with Vaughan and Shelley, we find a poem mimetic of the vertiginous path of water from on high before it descends to resolve into a pool below—and again we follow the course of streams and rivers as they move on through the landscape. Vaughan begins with visual effects of lineation and accompanying changes in speed. Shelley sets out with sublime flights of focus toward the unseen prior forces shaping the topography. In contrast, Hopkins has each of his first three stanzas depict a specific motion; each has multiple possible referents that bridge the worlds of water, plants, and animals. Hopkins loads his usual stress marks into the first two stanzas, punctuating the description of the water's fall with their rhythm.

The opening plunges us into the scene. The description of the burn or creek as "horseback brown" seems merely descriptive of color until the enjambment to the next line when we plummet "rollrock high road roaring down" with the verb descriptive of both the burn and animal motion.

What happens next? This plunge with its foaming waters leads in the second stanza to the circling pool of froth at the base of the waterfall. So much exact material description and yet here a personification of Despair is introduced by negation: it is the abstraction Despair that appears, apparently out of the consciousness of the speaker, and is drowned by the circling ripples of the pool. In the next stanza Hopkins paints a set of visual images of the plant life at the edges of this base: the ferns, the heather, and the ash with its red berries—all wet with the dew of the waterfall's splashing. And then the closure, with its prayerful tribute, asking permission for the continuity of wilderness and water.

These are perhaps the most obvious features of the poem. But what draws our attention throughout is Hopkins's lexicon and its extraordinary sound play, full of plosives, fricative f's alone and in consonant blends, rolling r's, and increasingly voiced w's. In these sounds we can start to grasp the poem not as an ekphrastic landscape poem alone, but, to use Hopkins's own well-known term, an inscape. Catherine Phillips gives a helpful account of these words,[32] listed here by their line endings:

> 3. *coop*: perhaps a hollow "Rushing streams may be described as inscaped ordinarily in pillows—and upturned troughs."
> *comb*: water pouring over a rock so that it forms ridges.
> *lutes*: the architectural meaning applied to ridges of water, used here to suggest the appearance of grooves in the falling plane of water.
> 6. *twindles*: perhaps Lancashire dialect "twins"—the foam divides into two or doubles. Alternatively the verb may be a combination of "twine" (to coil) and "spindle" (to grow into a long, slender form).
> 9. *degged*: Lancashire dialect for "sprinkled," "bedewed."
> 11. *heathpacks*: heather.
> *Flitches*: stiff, browned fronds like thin strips of tree trunk.
> 12. *beadbonny ash*: mountain ash, which has masses of red berries in the autumn.

Phillips notes that two of these words, "twindles" and "degged," are in Lancashire dialect; "flitch" is an Old English word for a slab of meat (as it is in Thomas Hardy and even today in my home county of York, Pennsylvania); the OED says "beadbonny" (though it echoes Scots "bonny" for beautiful) is a Hopkins neologism.[33] Hopkins's lifelong interest in dialects and local terms, from the deep past to contemporary usage, is on full display here.

81

Yet the onward lexical rush of the poem lands on the plane of personification with *Despair*, its Latin root *de* indicating down, down from, from, off. The Old English *sped*, meaning luck or success, tied up with haste or speed, merges with the Latin *spes*, indicating hope. The terms spill from line to line and grow in resonance to the spaces and times of their origins.

A wild plant is one that grows without human intention, a weed a plant that is found beyond its place or otherwise in the wrong place. In his early diaries, in 1863, Hopkins could write about watching water surge through a lock creating and diminishing emerging forms: "a mass of yellowish boiling foam which runs down between the fans, and meeting covers the whole space of the lock-entrance. Being heaped up in globes and bosses and round masses the fans disappear under it," describing the "folded and doubled lines of foam [as] worse confounded."[34] On a previous visit to Lancashire, in 1871, an acquaintance had told him that the word "sail" means to circle round. Like the sailor Michel Serres, Hopkins felt this was "no tautology," for he linked it to "the double made in the water by the return current where at a spread of the stream caused by the bend or otherwise the set or stem of the river bears on one bank and sets the slacker water on its outside spinning with its friction and so working back upstream."[35] Here, too, Hopkins's attention turns from the motion of water to the motion of the whole in a dynamic relation.

Edges, fans, globes, bosses, lines, spreads, doubles, spinning, working back—these are features of a composition that is constantly dissolving. Elsewhere he wrote, in the third of his "Trio of Triolets," "the words are wild."[36] And the plea at the end of "Inversnaid" echoed as well to his fragment of a proposed poem,

## MOTION AND TURN: WATER'S WAYS

"O where is it, the wilderness?" that he mentioned in a letter to Robert Bridges two years before: "I have … something, if I cd only seize it, on the decline of wild nature, beginning somehow like this—O where is it, the wilderness."[37] This is the fragment:

> 'O where is it, the wilderness'
> O where is it, the wilderness,
> The wildness of the wilderness?
> Where is it, the wilderness?
>
> ———
>
> And wander in the wilderness;
> In the weedy wilderness,
> Wander in the wilderness.[38]

Shelley, Vaughan, and Hopkins separate what endures from what is eternal; what endures is the universe of things, those mysterious and present natural forms that surround us, forms given over to the senses, historical and intelligible as continuing presences to be valued. What is eternal lies in color, light, geometry, and rhythm. These experiences are unaffected by endurance: they visit us in myriad forms. They are necessary to poetry and they are necessary to waterfalls and glaciers if they are to go into the future as wet and wild, more than the rocks that undergird them. As a species, we have access not only to consciousness, but also to these experiences of pattern and surprise, pleasure and beauty, unbound to any specific forms, yet ever-potential, ever-inspiring. I do not know why.

# IV

## THE IMPERCEPTIBLE, OR WILDERNESS

L et's start with a poem:

> A light exists in Spring
> Not present on the Year
> At any other period —
> When March is scarcely here
>
> A Color stands abroad
> On solitary Fields
> That Science cannot overtake
> But Human Nature feels.
>
> It waits opon the Lawn,
> It shows the furthest Tree
> Opon the furthest Slope you know
> It almost speaks to you.
>
> Then as Horizons step
> Or Noons report away
> Without the Formula of sound,
> It passes and we stay —

*Poetry's Nature*. Susan Stewart, Oxford University Press. © Susan Stewart (2025).
DOI: 10.1093/9780192577689.003.0004

> A quality of loss
> Affecting our Content
> As Trade had suddenly encroached
> Opon a Sacrament —[1]

Emily Dickinson could not have known, in 1865, the quantitative speed of light, and yet here she's written a poem about the qualities of light's emergence, existence, and passing.

The poem is a good example of the kind of response to nature I mentioned in my third lecture, quoting Hans Jonas: "a type of experience which involves 'impressions of reflection' in addition to those of 'sensation'; i.e., they involve the subject's awareness of his own inward mode of affectedness ... as an integral part-content of the object-experience itself."[2] Throughout these lectures, I have underscored that poetry is a liminal art; that is, an embodied art emergent in time, an art practiced between the material and abstraction and at the edge of, in an encounter with, the limits of our senses. The question of the relations between particularity and abstraction was perhaps most succinctly stated by Dickinson herself when she wrote:

> "Faith" is a fine invention
> For Gentlemen who *see!*
> But Microscopes are prudent
> In an Emergency![3]

Dickinson reminds us that phenomena are viewed in time—that unlike the atemporal domain of faith, phenomena are bound to moments, if not always to emergencies.

In "A light exists in Spring," she has been moved by her realizations about a seasonal moment, the light on the cusp of March—her sense that the quality of loss is like the feeling we might have if something sacred were overtaken by predetermined, calculating, interest. The poem demonstrates so well how inner experience is affected by outer experience and how particulars literally can shed light on abstractions.

Yet the work goes beyond its poignant and pointed ending, which might be read as one of many examples of Dickinson's disenchantment with institutionalized religion. For this work is also a study in, and a reflection upon, what human nature can feel in response to an encounter with aspects of nature that are imperceptible, things that "almost speak" to us—that is, the unobservable and unspecifiable, and yet the not quite ineffable. If we learn something about human nature in this poem, it is not that our measurements of the seasons (the year, the period, or noon), or our methods for determining value (from the powers of Science to the powers of commerce), or even our sense of spatial extension (the lawn, the tree, the slope, the horizon) can be used to frame that light we are feeling. The ground for apprehension here is intuition followed by a sensation of disappearance. We know the phenomenon only by a glimpse and its absence and the cause of that absence remain a mystery to us. If bird songs give us some sense of echo and response, these imperceptible experiences of nature are the testing ground for all that in life goes unsaid and all the animal thought and utterance that is closed to us.

These are domains that evade our intention, whether we use the terms of our cultures or the methods of our sciences: they are the wilderness—the place beyond law and certainty. We remember that the word "wilderness" has its etymology in words designated spaces outside of cultivation—barren, savage, unavailable. It is not as if these spaces were abandoned or proved themselves poor for habitation—they are, from the outset, other. Just as a weed is a plant in the wrong place, beyond the gardener's will and powers of naming, so on a much larger scale, jungle and deep forest are replete with unnamed, invisible species, and vast spaces of desert and sea do not lend themselves easily to cartography, let alone geometry. The unobservable aspects of the cosmos, like the myriad unknown processes of our own bodies, challenge our categories of understanding. As the concept of infinity gives us an intuition of time without limit, so does the concept of wilderness open our sense of extension to absolute space. The wilderness is a reserve or surplus. It is no doubt good for our mental health to picture it afar, yet in truth it is quite near; it is wherever our knowledge ends, even when we are not aware that we have reached that boundary.

I would like to turn in this final lecture to this kind of experience of nature and our own nature—the experience of phenomena at the limits of our powers of seeing, hearing, and proprioception. These experiences can come to us, as Dickinson's has, through a feeling that something overwhelming surrounds us and has no edge or that something has been withdrawn or has been or will be withheld. The imperceptible weighs upon us at the greatest intensity of sense experience—in the onslaught of storms and natural disasters that has long been the domain of the sublime at its best and pain at its worst. Or it weighs on us as an insensible absence, either beyond a frontier or as a prior felt presence.

When nature surrounds us with its fullest powers, we acknowledge that its forces are ungraspable, that we find ourselves swamped, the vertical halting the horizontal: we cannot absorb what is before and around us. In poetry addressing these situations the fundamental problem of representing the force of external perception upon inner experience finds its analogy in the situation of observing natural violence from a position of safety or imagining a position of safety in the midst of turmoil. The poet therefore often draws a sharp contrast between the outdoors and the indoors, the scene of experience and the scene of writing, the powers of external nature and the consequences for the inner life. As Robert Burns wrote in his commonplace book in 1784: "There is scarcely any earthly object gives me more—I do not know if I should call it pleasure—but something which exalts me, something which enraptures me—than to walk in the sheltered side of a wood ... in a cloudy winter day, and hear the stormy wind howling among the trees, and raving over the plain. It is my best season for devotion: my mind is wrapt up in a kind of enthusiasm to *Him*, who ... 'walks on the wings of the wind'."[4]

We can think, too, of the anonymous lyric known as "O western wind," which survives in a Tudor part-book, with accompanying musical notation in a minor key:

> Westron wynde when wyll thow blow
> the smalle rayne downe can Rayne
> Cryst yf my love were in my Armys
> And I yn my bed Agayne.

Is the speaker on a journey? At sea in need of a wind to move a sail? There are many varied interpretations of this song, but wherever the speaker is, the location of the poem is not near the speaker's bed, and the gentle western wind and gentle small rain are being asked to create the conditions where reunion with the love and reunion with the bed, in that order, might follow.[5]

POETRY'S NATURE

Michael Drayton's 1606 "An Ode Written in the Peake" tells us that even "Amongst the Mountaines bleak / Expos'd to Sleet and Raine," "The Muse" of poetry are still "in ure"—that is, in practice.[6] These poems seem to be extreme instances of the situation we encountered in much Occitan and troubadour-derived verse where the external world either mirrors or stands in contrast to the feelings of the speaker. Such poems do so literally when they are addressing the wind through the breathing syllables of their own inspiration.

If we look at some aspects of two poems about storms that are two hundred years apart we find many similarities with regard to divergences between inner and outer weather and a corresponding loss of particulars. By 1713 Anne Finch had completed a poem on the great storm of 1703. Her title was "A Pindarick Poem Upon the Hurricane in November 1703, referring to this Text in Psalm 148. ver.8. Winds and Storms fulfilling his Word. With a HYMN compos'd of the 148th PSALM Paraphras'd."[7]

From its title forward, the poem contrasts the specificity of this particular hurricane in time, and the impossibility of actually seeing it before it has passed, to the timeless notion from Psalm 148 that winds and storms fulfill the Word of God. The week-long storm began on November 24 and passed over Central and Southern England. It killed more than 8,000 people, wrecked dozens of ships at sea, including many vessels of the Royal Navy, destroyed more than 30,000 trees, and toppled thousands of chimneys.

Finch's opening lines, necessarily spoken in the past tense by a speaker safe to speak, are addressed to the winds and state "you have obey'd, you WINDS, that must fulfill / The Great Disposer's righteous Will." Although she will attempt to take the measure of the storm, she also declares in the opening of her ode that

90

## THE IMPERCEPTIBLE, OR WILDERNESS

"undistinguish'd was your Prey"—that the storm did not deal in the domains of names, places, and numbers that the speaker necessarily will bring forward as she enumerates the damage left in its wake. The ode wavers between narrative and the deictic depiction of scenes framed by "now." At its close, Finch revisits the question of cause and, like many of her era, underscores the storm as an act of God. Human greatness, titles, and forms cannot address the force of providential storms.

> They are only safe, whom He alone defends.
> Then let to Heaven our general Praise be sent,
> Which did our farther Loss, our total Wreck prevent.
> And as our Aspirations do ascend,
>
> Let every Thing be summon'd to attend;
> And let the Poet *after God's own Heart*
> Direct our Skill in that sublimer part,
> And our weak Numbers mend!

This type of reflexive gesture regarding her own meter is typical of Finch's poems: in her more well-known ode to the spleen, for example, she describes how the spleen is attacking her as she writes, saying "I feel my Verse decay, and my crampt Numbers fail."[8] Here her numbers convey, too, a quantitative account of the storm's destruction: mentioning solitary trees and those whose "numbers form'd a wood." And at several points she makes the numbers a quality of the storm as well:

> even the lightest Things,
> As the minuter parts of Air,
> When Number to their Weight addition brings,
> Can, like the small, but numerous Insects Stings,
> Can, like th' assembl'd Winds, urge Ruin and Despair.

The transposition of numbers across objects, wind, and the poem itself underscores the boundary-breaking work of the storm. As she describes grand architectural structures with "deep Foundations" coming down "at once," she records the uncanny effect of artificial ornaments returned to their natural referents:

> Now down at once comes the superfluous Load,
> The costly Fret-work with it yields,
> Whose imitated Fruits and Flow'rs are strew'd,
> Like those of real Growth o'er the Autumnal Fields.

Artifacts of human making, expensively created, will not grow again without human hands to recreate them. Meanwhile, however, what she calls "real growth" in the autumnal fields, has the invisible capacity of self-renewal.

More than two hundred and fifty years later, what we perceive as the threshold between nature and culture is breached as well in Theodore Roethke's poem, "The Storm: *Forio d'Ischia*" from his 1964 book *The Far Field*.[9] In contrast to Finch's retrospective and surveying account, Roethke gives us a perspective from inside the experience of the storm. It is a long poem; for our purposes, I will focus on only the final section:

> 3
> We creep to our bed, and its straw mattress.
> We wait; we listen.
> The storm lulls off, then redoubles,
> Bending the trees half-way down to the ground,
> Shaking loose the last wizened oranges in the orchard,
> Flattening the limber carnations.
>
> A spider eases himself down from a swaying light-bulb,
> Running over the coverlet, down under the iron bedstead.

THE IMPERCEPTIBLE, OR WILDERNESS

The bulb goes on and off, weakly.
Water roars into the cistern.

We lie closer on the gritty pillow,
Breathing heavily, hoping—
For the great last leap of the wave over the breakwater,
The flat boom on the beach of the towering sea-swell,
The sudden shudder as the jutting sea-cliff collapses,
And the hurricane drives the dead straw into the living
    pine-tree.

Such a sharp contrast emerges between the storm and the still interior, where our undistracted attention can follow the progress of a spider moving from a light bulb to the coverlet to the floor, then return to the bulb. The speaker can hear his own breathing and the redoubled storm shaking the fruit from trees, flattening carnations, the roar of water in the cistern.

Yet the most vivid and violent description of the storm comes in the final four lines. We almost don't notice that the last leap of the wave, the boom on the beach, the collapsing sea-cliff are only hopes. Because these closing images are taking place in the imagination of the speaker, lying on his pillow, the final image of dead straw driven into the living pine-tree has an uncanny force. We must carry over our knowledge from the start of the section: the bed has a straw mattress. With horror, we realize that the interior of the bed now would be outside in the tree. The storm itself has conveyed the metaphor—the collapse of life and death, an apocalyptic vision of an interior turned inside out, an exterior turned outside in, and behind that, remembering the domains of straw and pines, the field become forest and forest become field. The poem brings us totally within the mind of the speaker—we can share his or her vision only through the poem. Here, as with Finch, the quality of finality of form that the poem promises is a stay against, or remedy for, the chaos of formlessness that nature has presented.

In considering some of the poles of imperception—from the abstraction of nature's fury to the blurring of the close-up, we recognize that there is a continuity between clarity and confusion in our apprehension of phenomena; the visual and auditory fields appear before us with no inherent logic beyond our conventions of seeing and hearing; tactility in turn unfolds in time and is open to surprise. In his late life remarks on Whitehead's philosophy, Merleau-Ponty translated Whitehead's aphorism "nature has a ragged edge" as nature is "en lambeaux," "nature is in tatters."[10] It is always a fragment of nature that we engage as individuals and as a species. And yet, whether we call it intuition or something else, we glimpse or sense something of what is beyond us.

In this manner, each perception of nature is a perception of detail, and an inherent paradox of part–whole relations is intrinsic to such perception. The closer we look, the more abstract is the detail; the process reveals the metonymy involved in all perception and the ways we counter the always potential infinity of detail with gestures of synthesis and analogical thinking.

When John Clare wrote of the clock a clay's point of view, we remember he described:

> While green grass beneath me lies
> Pearled wi' dew like fishes eyes[11]

The meter pulls us forward, but the complexity of the simile and implicit analogy here is wonderfully mind-boggling. We can ask:

THE IMPERCEPTIBLE, OR WILDERNESS

does "like fishes eyes" modify the lying pearled or only the dew? Dew is like the eyes of fishes. The eyes of fishes are pearled. Dew is the agent of the pearling of grass, but what is the agent of the pearling of fish's eyes? And how does a ladybug come to know the look of fish's eyes? For that matter, how does the poet imagine the repertoire of the ladybug's metaphors? We have crossed the boundaries of earth and water and as well the boundaries of reality and imagination.

Detail is something we notice, first in its particularity or often, as we keep noticing, in a particularity becoming part of a whole or perhaps a pattern. Detail can be essential to form, as in an elegance that would characterize each and all details; or it can be an ornament, as in an object stripped of its details. In other words, it may be essence or it may be supplement and supplements can go rogue. Paradigmatic studies of the aesthetics of detail have emphasized the cultural significance of detail—I am thinking especially of the distinguished work by Naomi Schor on detail in the nineteenth-century novel and Svetlana Alpers's work on Golden Age Dutch painting.[12] Schor argues that detail comes to be associated with a refined femininity. Alpers shows us that the arts of describing stem from a visual culture driven by interest in material arts and within a milieu of materialist values. In both studies, detail is one of the tools of realism in representation.

Nevertheless, at a certain point, the closer we look, the more likely we are to be observing abstractions such as shape and color. Indeed, perhaps the relation of detail and pattern is another dimension of the power of detail to generate abstraction—to lift out and transpose expectations and thoughts from the concrete particulars of our sense experience. Furthermore, in looking at representations of nature in works of art, we become aware of another aspect of the cultural significance of detail—nature has no detail or ornaments. If nature is in tatters, everything is a part.

The question then becomes what use is the concept of *natura* as a whole? We can think again of how Cartesian and Spinozan ideas about nature as synonymous with the properties of an infinite God were greatly influential up until the time of Kant. In this frame, the finite is imminently present in the infinite; finitude is the drawing of the finite from the powers of an infinite being. But gradually this account becomes self-contradicting: the phenomena of nature are not essences or products, but rather active forces themselves that continue to produce new forms, with consequences for our sense of nature as a whole and for ourselves as living beings. Kant had introduced a kind of Copernican revolution in thought about nature by placing human consciousness at the center of the concept. We have no access to *natura naturans*, only to the phenomena that appear to our senses. In this way at the turn of the nineteenth century, *natura naturata* largely came to replace the priority of *natura naturans*. Even so, Spinoza's ideas about the metamorphoses of nature passed into the thought and practice of Goethe, who recorded in 1795 that he was reading Spinoza with Frau von Stein. He explained that he found Spinoza "very near" and added that while he had not read every word, he could conclude: "the complete architecture of [Spinoza's] intellectual system stood before me."[13]

The American transcendentalists go on to inherit, via Goethe, a mixed legacy of Spinozan interest in the infinite and Kantian attention to the living forms of phenomena. Although he was sometimes given to writing hymns to "Nature" with a capital N, Ralph Waldo Emerson took from Goethe a notion that the

THE IMPERCEPTIBLE, OR WILDERNESS

naturing activities of nature were everywhere evident. Linking the creativity of the natural world to the creativity of his work as a poet, Emerson asked "why should we not participate in the invention of nature?"[14] Here the humanist and Romantic notion of nature as constructed becomes key to the work of poetics as making, even if the work of art expresses a finality and begins in conscious intent rather than in responses to appearances alone.[15] In Emerson's 1841 poem, "The Snow-Storm," we find a paradigmatic meditation upon the free self-forming work of nature and human imitations.[16]

The Snow-Storm

Announced by all the trumpets of the sky,
Arrives the snow, and, driving o'er the fields,
Seems nowhere to alight: the whited air
Hides hill and woods, the river, and the heaven,
And veils the farmhouse at the garden's end.
The sled and traveller stopped, the courier's feet
Delayed, all friends shut out, the housemates sit
Around the radiant fireplace, enclosed
In a tumultuous privacy of storm.

Come see the north wind's masonry.
Out of an unseen quarry evermore
Furnished with tile, the fierce artificer
Curves his white bastions with projected roof
Round every windward stake, or tree, or door.
Speeding, the myriad-handed, his wild work
So fanciful, so savage, nought cares he
For number or proportion. Mockingly,
On coop or kennel he hangs Parian wreaths;
A swan-like form invests the hidden thorn;
Fills up the farmer's lane from wall to wall,

> Maugre the farmer's sighs; and at the gate,
> A tapering turret overtops the work.
> And when his hours are numbered, and the world
> Is all his own, retiring, as he were not,
> Leaves, when the sun appears, astonished Art
> To mimic in slow structures, stone by stone,
> Built in an age, the mad wind's night-work,
> The frolic architecture of the snow.

Even the form of blank verse is an homage to the snow's white work. The first nine-line stanza blasts upon the scene with aural images of thunder and by line 5 the particles of snow are thick enough to have created a veil. Against all this motion, Emerson introduces a series of tiny genre paintings of human scenes of stillness and interiority. In a line that Emily Dickinson treasured, the storm's conditions create for "the housemates" a "tumultuous privacy."[17] The stanza break that follows seems itself an allusion to the whiteout conditions of the storm.

The second stanza's nineteen lines are framed by the imperative of "Come see"—the opening of the poem had drawn our eyes to the sky and over a vast landscape before directing us through the garden, to the house, and in to the fireplace. Now we see, not vistas, but particulars. The phrase "Come see" evokes a scene viewed through a window. Yet immediately Emerson underscores the "unseen quarry" out of which the event of the storm has arisen. The fierce artificer, situated beyond our perception, aided by the north wind's myriad hands, works with complete freedom: "nought cares he for number or proportion," for he is the source of all invisible rules of number and proportion.

THE IMPERCEPTIBLE, OR WILDERNESS

In Emerson's transposition of Spinoza and Kant, *natura naturans* moves from the unformed blur of the storm's white consequences in the first stanza to mocking manifestations of human architectural achievement—Parian wreaths, those excellent white marble decorations celebrating human excellence; swan-like forms, tapering turrets. Each masks an element of the scene: in turn, the dwellings of animals, the humble thorn, a farmer's lane and gate. "The Snow-Storm" compares the progress of the storm with the progress of the diurnal. The poem begins in daylight, passes through a night, and ends with the reappearance of the sun. In this sense it surveys the genres of the nocturne and the alba. As we've seen with earlier examples, the poem, as an art made in time, addresses the duration of natural phenomena as events.

The poem leaves us with astonished Art, bound to imitate in stone what the snow has left with such frenzied freedom and grace: imitations in snow of human forms. Or at least, that is what we make of what we see. It is significant that these details are ornaments, not signs of necessity but of excess and choice. Meanwhile, the poem is hinged on two words, archaic to Emerson as they are to us: *maugre* and *frolic*—northern, French and German words respectively. *Maugre* here means despite, but carries over its medieval connotations of necessity and suffering malice. And *frolic*, its opposite, indicates the freedom of play and merry-making. The sighing farmer, and human architects, are bound to the slow work of ages: the storm's mad work, the speaker contends, can be done in a night. We notice that, as an inspired and made thing, a poem, belying its own hidden quarries and concealing its labor or revision, is here closer to the work of the wind. Despite its invisibility, the wind, like our inner wind, the breath, is felt and its effects are consequential.

In contrast, a wave presents a momentarily visible and paradigmatic moving object, one never itself, but rather abstracted from the progress of its motion. Indeed, the sea or ocean presents an especially rich arena for the maker of nature poems. It seems to me that one reason that we North American poets have something like a genre of the seashore poem is because our tradition has arisen between the blank, but ever-changing, canvas of the sea and the unintelligible polymorphic detail of the spectacle of impenetrable forests. Henry David Thoreau expressed in his essay "Walking" (published in June of 1862, a month after his death on May 6) similar thoughts as he struggled to think about the translation of English tradition into a new North American literature. He wrote: "English literature, from the days of the minstrels to the Lake Poets,—Chaucer and Spenser and Milton, and even Shakespeare, included,—breathes no quite fresh and, in this sense, wild strain. It is an essentially tame and civilized literature, reflecting Greece and Rome. Her wilderness is a green wood,—her wild man a Robin Hood. There is plenty of genial love of Nature, but not so much of Nature herself … Where is the literature which gives expression to Nature?" he asks, and then answers, "I do not know of any poetry to quote which adequately expresses this yearning for the Wild."[18] Putting to the side his stereotypical views, let's briefly consider several further works from the United States in this light, beginning with work that dates to Thoreau's own moment.

At the heart of Walt Whitman's "Sea-Drift" passages in *Leaves of Grass* stand a trio of interrelated poems: situated on the beach,

THE IMPERCEPTIBLE, OR WILDERNESS

looking down into the sea, and on to the beach again. The first is "On the Beach at Night," a poem depicting a child and her father looking up to the autumn sky, observing the dynamic between fleeting, or "ravening," dark clouds, and the fixed light of Jupiter, the Pleiades, and the "vast immortal suns" and "long enduring pensive moons." The second and third poems are "The World below the Brine" and, returning to the location of the first poem, "On the Beach at Night Alone."[19]

As the sequence begins by looking up at the incommensurable motions of clouds and stars, the eleven-line poem "The World below the Brine" looks down to create a catalog of perceived phenomena on the one hand and imagined or thought abstractions on the other.

> The World below the Brine
>
> The world below the brine,
> Forests at the bottom of the sea, the branches and leaves,
> Sea-lettuce, vast lichens, strange flowers and seeds, the thick tangle, openings, and pink turf,
> Different colors, pale gray and green, purple, white, and gold, the play of light through the water,
> Dumb swimmers there among the rocks, coral, gluten, grass, rushes, and the aliment of the swimmers,
> Sluggish existences grazing there suspended, or slowly crawling close to the bottom,
> The sperm-whale at the surface blowing air and spray, or disporting with his flukes,
> The leaden-eyed shark, the walrus, the turtle, the hairy sea-leopard, and the sting-ray,
> Passions there, wars, pursuits, tribes, sight in those ocean-depths, breathing that thick-breathing air, as so many do,

> The change thence to the sight here, and to the subtle air
>   breathed by beings like us who walk this sphere,
> The change onward from ours to that of beings who walk
>   other spheres.

The initiating list of plant forms begins with a metaphor—a forest with branches and leaves, followed by the forms of sea-lettuce and lichens. The series becomes more and more vague, despite its specificity dissolving into flowers, seeds, and a list of "different colors," the play of light through the water.

And then Whitman turns to those animals depending upon this plant life: to dumb swimmers amid rocks and coral, gluten grass, and rushes, and "aliments" or other plant food of such swimmers. This survey of the bottom, moving between opacity, cloudedness, and transparency, ends with the speaker noting "sluggish existences" with their slow crawling speed. And then Whitman goes to the surface, describing the sperm-whale, shark, walrus, turtle, hairy sea leopard, and the sting ray. Here too Whitman falls into abstraction, pulling back to note the agon of the ocean depths—the passions, wars, pursuits, tribes, of these sea creatures. As he comes back "to the sight here" and to air that accommodates human life, he draws a pair of lines beginning "The change thence" and "The change onward." He imagines the evolution of "beings like us who walk this sphere," and, like Giordano Bruno before him, "beings who walk other spheres." Following the shift between fleeting clouds and fixed stars in "On a Beach at Night" "The World below the Brine" moves from specific details to the abstraction of the heavens. Representing the world below the brine is impossible in multiple ways— impossible to view, impossible to totalize. Our fundamental

## THE IMPERCEPTIBLE, OR WILDERNESS

difficulties are not merely those of invisibility and the difficulty of penetrating the sea's surface, but simply our need to breathe. Our sphere is the sphere of the breathable air by which we live and as well make poems.

Here is the close to the sequence, "On the Beach at Night Alone."

On the Beach at Night Alone,

On the beach at night alone,
As the old mother sways her to and fro singing her husky
    song,
As I watch the bright stars shining, I think a thought of the
    clef of the universes and of the future.
A vast similitude interlocks all,
All spheres, grown, ungrown, small, large, suns, moons,
    planets,
All distances of place however wide,
All distances of time, all inanimate forms,
All souls, all living bodies though they be ever so different,
    or in different worlds,
All gaseous, watery, vegetable, mineral processes, the
    fishes, the brutes,
All nations, colors, barbarisms, civilizations, languages,
All identities that have existed or may exist on this globe,
    or any globe,
All lives and deaths, all of the past, present, future,
This vast similitude spans them, and always has spann'd,
And shall forever span them and compactly hold and
    enclose them.

The old mother of the sea sways to and fro and sings her husky song. The clef or key to a musical composition provides the initiating terms and in fact the initial title for this work was "Clef

Poem." Whitman's implication is that the song of the sea is the key to *harmonia mundi* and as well the determination of all that will follow. The poem sets out, like planets on an orrery, the largest units of living, perceptible forms: the universe; worlds; processes; nations; and this globe and any globe.

Here "a vast similitude interlocks" all spheres, distances of place and time, souls of living bodies in all possible worlds, all forms of living processes, all categories of culture, all identities, all lives and deaths, past, present, and future. The final gesture out to space is turned inside out into a gesture of enclosure. The poem is a kind of treatise against difference and in the end it enacts the defining quality of infinity—the ability of a part to contain the whole. This was an idea that Whitman would have found in Fichte, whose theories of the interrelations of subjectivity and perception he noted with approval in his "Sunday Evening Lectures" on German metaphysics.[20]

Let's turn to a third seaside poem, Marianne Moore's "A Grave."

A Grave

Man looking into the sea,
taking the view from those who have as much right to it as
    you have to it yourself,
it is human nature to stand in the middle of a thing,
but you cannot stand in the middle of this;
the sea has nothing to give but a well excavated grave.
The firs stand in a procession, each with an emerald turkey-
    foot at the top,
reserved as their contours, saying nothing;

# THE IMPERCEPTIBLE, OR WILDERNESS

repression, however, is not the most obvious characteristic
    of the sea;
the sea is a collector, quick to return a rapacious look.
There are others besides you who have worn that look—
whose expression is no longer a protest; the fish no longer
    investigate them
for their bones have not lasted:
men lower nets, unconscious of the fact that they are
    desecrating a grave,
and row quickly away—the blades of the oars
moving together like the feet of water-spiders as if there
    were no such thing as death.
The wrinkles progress among themselves in a phalanx—
    beautiful under networks of foam,
and fade breathlessly while the sea rustles in and out of
    the seaweed;
the birds swim through the air at top speed, emitting cat-
    calls as heretofore—
the tortoise-shell scourges about the feet of the cliffs, in
    motion beneath them;
and the ocean, under the pulsation of lighthouses and
    noise of bell-buoys,
advances as usual, looking as if it were not that ocean in
    which dropped things are bound to sink—
in which if they turn and twist, it is neither with volition
    nor consciousness.[21]

Moore began the poem in 1919 and at one point she called it
"A Graveyard"—quite a different title. The aphoristic third and
fourth lines, "it is human nature to stand in the middle of a
thing, / but you cannot stand in the middle of this" are indebted
to a witticism made by Moore's mother. The two women were

looking out at the surf from a middle ledge of rocks on Monhegan Island after a storm when a man stood in front of them, blocking their view of the sea. "Don't be annoyed," her mother said, "It is human nature to stand in the middle of a thing."[22]

We cannot stand in the middle of the sea, as Moore reminds us, and we cannot stand in the middle of a process—the word comes up right away as she makes the pronouncement that the sea is a grave and turns our eyes back to the land where the silent firs stand in a procession. Moore explained to Ezra Pound in a letter of 1919 that addressed an early version of this poem, "any verse I have written, has been an arrangement of stanzas, each stanza being an exact duplicate of every other stanza."[23] Perhaps none of her poems have the form of a succession of waves more than this poem. The phenomena she describes remain on the surface except for the conjectured fish that no longer investigate the bones of the dead. Like Whitman and Emerson, she stays in the present tense: men lower nets; the wrinkles made by their oars progress under networks of foam; birds swim through the air; the tortoise-shell, all we can see of the tortoise, scourges about the feet of the cliffs, and the ocean advances as usual.

The shift from sea to ocean in the poem is significant—Moore, ever-careful in her use of terms, indicates the little-recognized and by definition amorphous difference between the sea, which is a body of water having some interface with land, and ocean, which is the general term for the great body of water that covers the earth. Seas are where land and ocean meet. In "A Grave" human beings look only into the sea—meanwhile, the ocean advances toward us. The sea is where human remains lie, but the ocean is the agent of the end of human volition and

THE IMPERCEPTIBLE, OR WILDERNESS

consciousness—that noumenal place where human being both begins and finds its limit.

I've chosen these poems by Emerson, Whitman, and Moore because they bear traces of Aristotelian techniques of observation, Spinozan ideas of the unity of nature, and the analogical thinking of transcendentalism itself. As North American East Coast poems, they also have a local affinity and vocabulary. Each of them is concerned with experiences and accounts of change within a world. And each addresses both the concept of an edge and the liminal kinds of noticing, between perception and thought, that take place at such an edge.

Yet in none of these poems do we find the structure M. H. Abrams described in his classic study of the uses of the pathetic fallacy in the greater British and European Romantic lyrics[24]—for example, in Giacomo Leopardi's "L'Infinito" or, as we saw, in Shelley's "Mont Blanc." In such lyrics, a first person speaker circles out to the natural, often sublime, world, then returns to his or her own consciousness in light of nature, and finally returns to nature with heightened, often exalted, insight.

The structure of each of these North American works, in contrast, stays very close in appearance and temporality to the phenomenon addressed. Nature is an object of the senses, but it remains self-contained; it is independent of, as Moore writes, our volition and consciousness. And, bitter truth, it also is independent of our moral and aesthetic values. As Nietzsche wrote in a critique of the Stoics in *Beyond Good and Evil*, nature is "wasteful beyond measure, indifferent beyond measure, without purposes and consideration, without mercy and justice, fertile and desolate and uncertain at the same time." He added, "imagine indifference itself as a power."[25]

POETRY'S NATURE

At a moment when we like to remind ourselves we are part of nature, and nature part of us, and when the triumph of materialism seems so complete that we are willing to consider persons, animals, and other phenomena of nature as objects, even toys, of our attitudes and aspirations, these works of art in time, overdetermined in their relation to the particulars of nature, might alert us to the limits of our awareness. And they might direct us to an acknowledgment that nature is unlikely to be sentimental about either our perceptual failures or, it is looking probable, our vanishing. Yet Nietzsche should not have the last word, for his perspective is naive in its own way. Nature may well be without consideration and measure, indifferent and unintelligible. If we nevertheless envision ourselves as part of nature, each of these qualities becomes both restored and particular. Kant suggested in his passages on teleology in the *Critique of the Power of Judgment* that even if we cannot be certain of nature's purpose, we have the ability to imagine it has a purpose. In his distinction between the productive and reproductive imagination, he proposed a link between nature's creativity and our own that is indeed founded in such imaginative work. His thinking invites us to imagine that we, too, have a purpose—to foster that same imagination and to place ourselves within creation as more than predators and less than gods.

# NOTES

## Lecture I

1. These lectures are limited in scope to a continuous tradition of Western aesthetics; given the constraints of my expertise, it would be more than presumptuous to draw "universal" conclusions about the philosophy of nature and any attempt at a survey would be merely anecdotal. For a rich theoretical discussion of the differences between totemic and animistic belief systems in relation to concepts of nature, see Philippe Descola, "Constructing natures: symbolic ecology and social practice," in *Nature and Society: Anthropological Perspectives*, ed. Philippe Descola and Gísli Pálsson (London: Routledge, 1996), 82–102. Descola argues: "I am reluctant to adopt the relativist position because, among other reasons, it presupposes the existence of what needs to be established. If every culture is considered as a specific system of meanings arbitrarily coding an unproblematic natural world, which everywhere possesses all the features that our own culture attributes to it, then not only does the very cause of the nature-culture(s) division remain unquestioned, but, declarations to the contrary notwithstanding, there can be no escape from the epistemological privilege granted to western culture, the only one whose definition of nature serves as the implicit measuring rod for all others" (84–5). He raises the possibility that a nature/culture dichotomy can be a heuristic for classification but is not ontologically significant. Carlo Severi has written a powerful analysis of intensification and animation in relation to representation in his *Capturing Imagination: A Proposal for an Anthropology of Thought*, trans. Catherine V. Howard, Matthew Carey, Eric Bye, Ramon Fonkoue, and Joyce Suechun Cheng (Chicago, IL: Hau Books, University of Chicago Press, 2018). Su Hui's and Lin Yinbo's "A Comparative Study on the Man–Nature Relationship and Its Presentation in Chinese and British

## NOTES

Nature Poetry" explores some of the ways tenets of Taoism and Confucianism have affected the development of Chinese nature poems. Hui and Yinbo, "A Comparative Study," *Forum for World Literature Studies* 7, no. 4 (December 2015): 633–42.

2. For further reading: "'Nature' as Aesthetic Norm," in Arthur O. Lovejoy, *Essays in the History of Ideas* (Baltimore, MD: The Johns Hopkins University Press, 1948), 69–77; "Some Meanings of 'Nature'," Appendix, in Arthur O. Lovejoy and George Boas, *Primitivism and Related Ideas in Antiquity* (Baltimore, MD: The Johns Hopkins University Press, 1935), 447–56. On the genitive aspect of *phusis* and its gradual transformation into a notion of process, see Pierre Hadot, *The Veil of Isis: An Essay on the History of the Idea of Nature*, trans. Michael Chase (Boston, MA: Harvard University Press, 2006), 17–21.

3. "The Receptacle of Becoming," *Timaeus* (48E–49A) in *Plato's Cosmology: The Timaeus of Plato*, trans. Francis M. Cornford (New York: Macmillan), 48–53.

4. Plato, *Sophist*, 265E, trans. Seth Bernadete (Chicago, IL: University of Chicago Press, 1984), II.64–5.

5. Hadot, *The Veil of Isis*, 201, 57.

6. Aristotle, *Physics*, Book II, trans. R. P. Hardie and R. K. Gaye, in *The Basic Works of Aristotle*, ed. Richard McKeon (New York: Random House, 1941), 236–52.

7. *Nicomachean Ethics*, Book VI, 1140a, 10–16. See Roger French, "Aristotle and the Nature of Things," in *Ancient Natural History* (London: Routledge, 1994), 5–67, for helpful context regarding Aristotle's views of the living and nonliving, motion, and process.

8. Spinoza wrote, "I wish here to explain, what we should understand by nature viewed as active (*natura naturans*), and nature viewed as passive (*natura naturata*). I say to explain, or rather call attention to it, for I think that, from what has been said, it is sufficiently clear, that by nature viewed as active we should understand that which is in itself, and is conceived through itself, or those attributes of substance, which express eternal and infinite essence, in other words God, in so far as he is considered as a free cause.

By nature viewed as passive I understand all that which follows from the necessity of the nature of God, or of any of the attributes

# NOTES

of God, that is, all the modes of the attributes of God, in so far as they are considered as things which are in God, and which without God cannot exist or be conceived." *Ethics*, in Benedict de Spinoza, *On the Improvement of the Understanding, the Ethics, Correspondence*, trans. R. H. M. Elwes (New York: Dover, 1955), 68–9, Part I, prop. 29. Aquinas uses "natura naturans" (nature naturing) in the *Summa Theologica* I–II, question 85, a. 6, and *De Divinis Nominibus* 4. 21. [See the *New English Translation of St. Thomas Aquinas's Summa Theologiae (Summa Theologica)* by Alfred J. Freddoso, University of Notre Dame, www3.nd.edu/~afreddos/summa-translation/TOC-part1-2.htm, 589, and https://documentacatholicaomnia.eu/03d/1225-1274,_Thomas_Aquinas,_In_Dionysii_de_Divinis_Nominibus,_LT. pdf, 62–4.] For the scholastics, *natura naturans* is God as maker; *natura naturata*, the maker's creations. Spinoza scholars continue to differ in their interpretations of whether Spinoza separates divine *natura naturans* from the modes and forms of *natura naturata* or whether *natura naturans* is an all-encompassing wholeness within which the active part, *natura naturata*, is subsumed. See Frank Lucash, "Spinoza's Two Views of Substance," in *Dialogue: Revue canadienne de philosophie* 50, no. 3 (September 2011): 537–55.

9. Immanuel Kant, "On the ground of the distinction of all objects in general into *phenomena* and *noumena*" [A235/B294–A250/B315], in *The Critique of Pure Reason*, eds. Paul Guyer and Allen Wood (Cambridge: Cambridge University Press, 1998), 338–65.

10. A. N. Whitehead, *Science and the Modern World* (New York: Macmillan, 1925), 74. See also "Nature Lifeless," Lecture Seven of Whitehead's *Modes of Thought* (New York: Free Press, Macmillan), 127–47.

11. As Isabelle Stengers explains, Whitehead is not "negotiating in a finer way what will be 'saved,' [or] attributed to nature. Everything is going to have to be saved together, at the same time, and by the same means." Whitehead will drop the question of "what" perception perceives to address the problem of knowledge at the heart of "how" perception perceives. Isabelle Stengers, *Thinking with Whitehead: A Free and Wild Creation of Concepts*, trans. Michael Chase (Cambridge, MA: Harvard University Press, 2014), 40–1.

12. Whitehead, *Modes of Thought*, 164.

# NOTES

13. For a layperson such as myself, some useful books for learning about the interrelatedness of life forms and the earth itself as a living phenomenon include Lynn Margulis and Dorion Sagan, *What Is Life?* (Berkeley, CA: University of California Press, 1995) (the title is an homage to Erwin Schrödinger's seminal work of the same name from 1944 arguing for physics and chemistry as tools for studying biology), a work particularly concerned with bacteria; Paul Nurse's *What Is Life?: Five Great Ideas in Biology* (New York: Norton, 2020), especially his successive chapters "Life as Chemistry" and "Life as Information" (55–108), a work particularly concerned with cell theory; Peter Godfrey-Smith's *Metazoa: Animal Life and the Birth of the Mind* (New York: Farrar Straus, 2020), a work particularly concerned with the evolutionary emergence of sentience. Simon Conway Morris's *Life's Solution: Inevitable Humans in a Lonely Universe* (Cambridge: Cambridge University Press, 2003) offers a far-reaching account of patterns in evolution, revealing how similar functional requirements even across far-flung species result in similar adaptations.

14. Carlo Rovelli, *Reality Is Not What It Seems: The Journey to Quantum Gravity*, trans. Simon Carnell and Erica Segre (New York: Riverhead Books, 2017), 135.

15. Steven Meyer, Introduction to the special issue "Whitehead Now," *Configurations* 13, no.1 (Winter 2005): 1–33: "Whitehead did invent 'creativity,' ... a term that quickly became so popular, so omnipresent, that its invention within living memory, and by Alfred North Whitehead of all people, quickly became occluded" (2).

16. Whitehead, *Science and the Modern World*, 108 and 116–17 (Wordsworth) and 118–23 (Shelley).

17. The sentence is Whitehead's, from his *Concept of Nature* (Cambridge: Cambridge University Press, 1920), 54.

18. R. B. Parkinson, *Voices from Ancient Egypt: An Anthology of Middle Kingdom Writings* (London: British Museum Press, 1991); *The Book of Songs: The Ancient Chinese Classic of Poetry*, trans. Arthur Waley (New York: Grove Press, 1996).

19. W. K. Wimsatt, "Verbal Style: Logical and Counterlogical," *PMLA* 65, no. 2 (March 1950): 5–20; "One Relation of Rhyme to Reason: Alexander Pope," *Modern Language Quarterly* 5, no. 3 (September 1944): 323–38.

# NOTES

20. *Shelley's Poetry and Prose*, ed. Donald Reiman (New York: Norton, 1977), 506.

21. W. K. Wimsatt, "Verbal Style": 10–11 (citing W. H. Auden, *The Poet's Tongue*, eds. Auden and John Garrett [London: G. Bell & Sons, 1935], vi), 20.

22. "The cuckoo comes in April, / he sings his song in May / He changes his tune in the middle of June / and then he flies away."

23. Issues of the historical context of the song, British Library MS Harley 978, Folio 11v, its relation to genres such as the spring-greeting *reverdie*, as well as its summer theme and possible allusions to cuckoldry, are addressed in James M. Dean, "Mood Imperative: The Cuckoo, the Latin Lyrics, and the 'Cuckoo Song'," *Philological Quarterly* 85, nos. 3, 4 (Summer, Fall 2006): 207–22; and G. H. Roscow, "What is 'Sumer Is Icumen In'?" *The Review of English Studies* 50, no. 198 (May 1999): 188–95. I follow the text used by Roscow, which is based on Carleton Brown's *English Lyrics of the XIIIth Century* (Oxford: Oxford University Press, 1932). Elizabeth Helsinger discusses the song in "Poem Into Song," *New Literary History* 46, no. 4 (Autumn 2015): 671–2.

24. Matthew Rowlinson discusses Descartes's choice of examples and their classical sources in "Onomatopoeia, Interiority, and Incorporation," *Studies in Romanticism* 57, no. 3 (Fall 2018): 433–4.

25. Heather Williams, "Birdsong and Singing Behavior," *Annals of the New York Academy of Sciences*, 1016, no. 1 (January 2006): 1–30.

26. E. O. Wilson, "Biophilia," in *E. O. Wilson*, ed. David Quammen (New York: Library of America, 1991), 75: "Life of any kind is infinitely more interesting than almost any conceivable variety of inanimate matter. The latter is valued chiefly to the extent that it can be metabolized into live tissue, accidentally resembles it, or can be fashioned into a useful and properly animated artifact. No one in his right mind looks at a pile of dead leaves in preference to the tree from which they fell. ... I have suggested that the urge to affiliate with other forms of life is to some degree innate, hence deserves to be called biophilia."

27. Richard d'A. Jensen explores these limits to similarities in his "Birdsong and the Imitation of Birdsong in the Music of the Middle Ages and the Renaissance," *Current Musicology* 40, no. 1 (January 1985): 50.

28. Erich D. Jarvis, "Evolution of Brain Pathways for Vocal Learning in Birds and Humans," in *Birdsong, Speech, and Language: Exploring the Evolution of*

## NOTES

*Mind and Brain*, eds. Johan J. Bolhuis and Martin Everaert (Cambridge, MA: MIT Press, 2013), 63–107. Further material from Jarvis's research can be found on his lab webpage: www.jarvislab.net. In *Life's Solution*, Conway Morris cites research by Marc Hauser and Peter Marler into homologies between bird subsong and human babbling as another instance of convergences: "a basic set of strategies that any species would be likely to employ if it embarks on the development of a system of communication based on learned signals" (252; quoting Hauser and Marler in *Phonological Development: Models, Research, Implications*, eds. C. A. Ferguson et al. [Timonium, MD: York Press, 1992], 669).

29. "The Woodlark," in *Gerard Manley Hopkins*, ed. Catherine Phillips (Oxford: Oxford University Press, 1986), 122. *The Journals and Papers of Gerard Manley Hopkins*, ed. Humphry House (London: Oxford University Press, 1959), 138.

30. These are Clare's terms, but we might note the resonance to Sarah Kay's exploration of a distinction between talking and singing birds in her pathbreaking study of the production and reception of Occitan troubadour songs. She distinguishes between "nightingales," troubadours who sang their original compositions, and "parrots," those who took up the original songs and quoted and commented upon them. Her study reveals many dimensions of the history of poetic song, not the least of which is the assignation of roles in literary production as analogous to, perhaps even mimetic of, a species distinction in the natural world. Sarah Kay, *Parrots and Nightingales: Troubadour Quotations and the Development of European Poetry* (Philadelphia, PA: University of Pennsylvania Press, 2013).

31. John Clare, "*The Progress of Rhyme*," 1824–43, printed in *The Midsummer Cushion*, eds. R. K. R. Thornton and Anne Tibble (Manchester: Mid-Northumberland Arts Group, Carcanet Press, 1990), 229.

32. Robert Stark, *Ezra Pound's Early Verse and Lyric Tradition: A Jargoner's Apprenticeship* (Edinburgh: Edinburgh University Press, 2012). Coleridge is quoted on p. 16.

33. Ezra Pound, *ABC of Reading* (London: Faber, 1951), 53–4.

34. Re these Provençal terms: "auzels" are birds; "chirms" indicates flocks. Pound, *Instigations* (New York: Boni and Liveright, 1920), 311. In *The Spirit of Romance* (New York: New Directions, 1968), based on the 1910 edition,

## NOTES

Pound translates these openings into prose: "Sweet clamor, cries, and lays and songs and vows do I hear of the birds, who in their Latin make prayers each to his mate, even as we here to those loved ladies whom our thoughts intend; and therefore I, who have set my thought upon the noblest, should make a chançon of fine workmanship above all the rest, where there be not a false word or a rhyme strained" (33).

35. Throughout, I refer to *The English and Scottish Popular Ballads*, ed. Francis James Child, in five volumes (New York: Dover, 1965).

36. Bertrand Harris Bronson, *The Traditional Tunes of the Child Ballads* (Princeton, NJ: Princeton University Press, 1959), 1:270.

37. Bess Lomax Hawes, "Folksongs and Function: Some Thoughts on the American Lullaby," *Journal of American Folklore* 87, no. 344 (April–June 1974), 140–8.

38. Roger D. Abrahams and George Foss, *Anglo-American Folksong Style* (Englewood Cliffs, NJ: Prentice-Hall, 1968), 18.

39. Albert Lord, *The Singer of Tales*, 3rd ed. (Milman Parry Collection of Oral Literature. Cambridge, MA: Harvard University Press, 2019).

40. Here Whitehead may again be of help. In his *Modes of Thought*, he writes: "When we come to mankind, nature seems to have burst through another of its boundaries. The central activity of enjoyment and expression has assumed a reversal in the importance of its diverse functionings. The conceptual entertainment of unrealized possibility becomes a major factor in human mentality ... it is the nature of feeling to pass into expression ... In mankind, the dominant dependence on bodily functioning seems still there. And yet the life of a human being receives its worth, its importance, from the way in which unrealized ideals shape its purposes and tinge its actions" (26–7).

41. Wallace Stevens, "The Course of a Particular," in *Stevens: Collected Poetry and Prose*, eds. Frank Kermode and Joan Richardson (New York: Library of America, 1997), 460.

42. Wallace Stevens to Robert Pack, April 14, 1955, in *Letters of Wallace Stevens*, ed. Holly Stevens (New York: Knopf, 1966), 881.

### Lecture II

1. Aristotle, *Poetics*, trans. Richard Janko (Indianapolis, IN: Hackett, 1987), 1451b1, p. 12.

## NOTES

2. Mina Gorji, *John Clare and the Place of Poetry* (Liverpool: Liverpool University Press, 2008), 123.

3. *The Later Poems of John Clare*, eds. Eric Robinson and David Powell, vol. 2 (Oxford: Clarendon Press, 1984), 611–12.

4. Hayden White, "The Structure of Historical Narrative," in *The Fiction of Narrative: Essays on History, Literature, and Theory, 1957–2007*, ed. Robert Doran (Baltimore, MD: The Johns Hopkins University Press, 2010), 119.

5. R. G. Collingwood, *The Idea of Nature* (New York: Oxford University Press, Galaxy Books, 1960), 25–6.

6. Augustine, *Confessions*, trans. R.S. Pine-Coffin (London: Penguin, 1962), 278.

7. See the discussion of "global coherence" in Christoph Unger, "A re-analysis of genre and its implications for pragmatics," in *Genre, Relevance, and Global Coherence: The Pragmatics of Discourse Type* (London: Palgrave Macmillan, 2006), 253–68.

8. Northrop Frye, *Anatomy of Criticism* (Princeton, NJ: Princeton University Press, 1957).

9. Gilles Deleuze, *Difference and Repetition*, trans. Paul Patton (London: Continuum, 2004) discusses this tension throughout.

10. Jessica Resvick gives a helpful account of Goethe's development of this concept out of his natural history writings and color theory into questions of aesthetics more generally, in "Wechsel-Dauer (Change-Constancy)," *Goethe-Lexicon of Philosophical Concepts* 3 (December 2022), https://doi.org/10.5195/glpc.2022.54.

11. Marcel Mauss, *Seasonal Variations of the Eskimo: A Study in Social Morphology*, in collaboration with Henri Beuchat, trans. James J. Fox (London: Routledge & Kegan Paul, 1979), 78–80. My thanks to Maria Sidorkina for turning me to this study.

12. See the recent essays on the phenomenology of the seasons in *The Seasons: Philosophical, Literary, and Environmental Perspectives*, eds. Luke Fischer and David Macauley (Albany, NY: SUNY Press, 2021). These seasonal phenomena associated with *kigo* are listed in David Macauley's essay, "The Four Seasons and the Rhythms of Place-Based Time" (31). The tradition of seasonal references in *haiku* is discussed in depth as well in William J. Higginson, *Haiku Seasons: Poetry of the Natural World* (Berkeley, CA: Stone Bridge Press, 2008).

## NOTES

13. These works can be found in translation in *Lark in the Morning: The Verses of the Troubadours*, ed. Robert Kehew, trans. Ezra Pound, W. D. Snodgrass, and Robert Kehew (Chicago, IL: University of Chicago Press, 2005).

14. Bodleian Summary Catalogue Vol. IV, 534–5. The poem and musical notation appear in Bodleian Douce 139 f 5.r. See Thomas C. Moser, "'And I Mon Waxe Wod': The Middle English 'Foweles in the Frith'," *PMLA* 102, no. 3 (May 1987): 326–37.

15. William Dunbar, "A Meditation in Winter," in *The Complete Works*, ed. John Conlee (Kalamazoo, MI: Medieval Institute Publications, 2004), no. 15, 51–2.

16. Gavin Douglas, *The Eneados, 1513*, Prologue to Book VII, ll. 155–62, in *Gavin Douglas's Translation of Virgil's* Aeneid, Vol. II, *Books I–VII*, eds. Priscilla Bawcutt with Ian Cunningham (Edinburgh: The Scottish Text Society, 2021), 244.

17. I thank Emily Lobb for her advice about this translation and for alerting me to the new Scottish Text Society editions listed above.

18. Rosemund Tuve, *Seasons and Months: Studies in a Tradition of Middle English Poetry* (Cambridge: D.S. Brewer, and Totowa, NJ: Rowman and Littlefield, 1933), 80.

19. Robert Durling, ed. and trans., *Petrarch's Lyric Poems: The Rime Sparse and Other Lyrics* (Cambridge, MA: Harvard University Press, 1976), 44–5.

20. Edmund Spenser, "Sonnet II," in *The Shorter Poems*, ed. Richard McCabe (London: Penguin, 1999), 388.

21. Sir Philip Sidney, *Selected Poems*, ed. Catherine Bates (London: Penguin, 1994), 99.

22. Vin Nardizzi, telling a "queerer version of generational and genealogical history, both sexual and textual," emphasizes that the sonnet "uneasily" yokes grafting guidebooks to human procreation and sees authorship as the most important form of reproduction in the sonnet. "Shakespeare's Penknife: Grafting and Seedless Generation in the Procreation Sonnets," *Renaissance and Reformation* 32, no. 1 (Winter 2009): 99.

23. The poem first appeared in William Hayley's *The Life and Posthumous Writings of William Cowper*, vol. 4 (Chichester: J. Seagrave for J. Johnson, 1806), 443–58. I have consulted as well the text of "Yardley Oak" in *Eighteenth-Century Poetry: An Annotated Anthology*, eds. David Fairer and

# NOTES

Christine Gerrard (Chichester: John Wiley, 2015), 629–33, which represents lines 144–66 that were crossed out in the manuscript in Cowper's hand that Hayley used. That manuscript is now in the Compton & Newton Museum.

24. In *The Life of William Cowper*, Thomas Wright writes: "Yardley Oak, the tree to which the poem is addressed, the hollow tree, the tree said by Cowper to be 22 feet 6 ½ inches in girth, is the one now called 'Cowper's Oak,' situated three miles from Weston, just beyond Kilwick Wood" (New York: Haskell House, 1892), 491. In a 1788 letter to his cousin Lady Hesketh, Cowper wrote: "I walked with him [Mr. Gifford] yesterday on a visit to an oak on the border of Yardley Chase, an oak which I often visit, and which is one of the wonders that I show to all who come this way, and have never seen it. I tell them all that it is a thousand years old, verily believing it to be so, though I do not know it. A mile beyond this oak stands another, which has from time immemorial been known by the name of Judith, and is said to have been an oak when my namesake the Conqueror first came hither." Cowper to Lady Hesketh, The Lodge, September 13 [or 18], 1788, in *The Correspondence of William Cowper, Arranged in Chronological Order*, ed. Thomas Wright, vol. 3 (London: Hodder & Stoughton, 1904), 317.

25. Quoted in headnote to Fairer and Gerrard, 545.

26. William Hayley, *Supplementary pages to the Life of Cowper: containing the additions made to that work on reprinting it in octavo* (Chichester: J. Seagrave for J. Johnson, 1806).

27. Richard N. Ringler, "The Genesis of Cowper's Yardley Oak," *English Language Notes* 5, no. 1 (1967): 27–32. Ringler discusses the numerous problems that have arisen in attempting to date the poem and describes Cowper's engagement with Erasmus Darwin's *Economy of Vegetation* as he prepared a review of the Darwin for *The Analytical Review*. See also the discussion of the Darwin influence in Charles Ryskamp, "Cowper and Darwin's *Economy of Vegetation*," *Harvard Library Bulletin* 9, no. 3 (Autumn 1957): 317–18. For Cowper's review itself: *The Analytical Review or History of Literature, Domestic and Foreign, on an Enlarged Plan*, vol. XV, January–May 1793 (London: J. Johnson, 1793), 287–93.

28. The most recent scholarly biography of Cowper remains James King, *William Cowper: A Biography* (Durham, NC: Duke University Press, 1986).

## NOTES

29. John Keats, *The Complete Poems*, ed. John Barnard, 3rd ed. (London: Penguin Books, 1988), 232.

30. Keats, *Endymion*, Book I, ll. 54–7, *Complete Poems*, 108.

31. Keats, *Complete Poems*, 217. Notes to the poem are on pp. 611–12. See as well Jeffrey N. Cox's notes to the poem in *Keats's Poetry and Prose* (New York: Norton, 2009), 105, notes 1–4. The text was first printed in 1829 in *The Literary Gazette* and soon after in *The Gem* and *The New Monthly Magazine*, and then in the Galignani edition of Keats's poems. Alvin Whitley, "The autograph of Keats's 'In Drear nighted December'," *Harvard Library Bulletin* 5, no. 1 (Winter 1951): 116–22. Duncan Wu, "'In Drear-Nighted December': The Newly Acquired KSMA Manuscript," *Keats-Shelley Review* 32, no. 1 (2018): 22–7, surveys the history of the texts in light of the recent purchase of a manuscript of the poem in the hand of John Hamilton Reynolds by the Keats–Shelley Museum in Rome. Wu reproduces the stemma made by Jack Stillinger for his study, *The Texts of Keats's Poems* (Cambridge, MA: Harvard University Press, 1974), 154. There is a lost rough draft of the poem and a contemporary printed text includes a revision, "to know the change and feel it" that may be the work of Richard Woodhouse. The fair copy in Keats's hand known as the "Bristol manuscript" shows this emendation. To my mind, the emendation is not a worthy replacement of the memorable "the feel of not to feel it," which certainly speaks eloquently to the lyric's wintry meditation on numbing. I have followed Stillinger's suggestion, confirmed by the KSMA manuscript, which follows the Bristol holograph, that the line is "Writhed not at passed joy."

32. Dryden, *The Spanish Fryar* (5.1.62ff), in eds. Vinton A. Dearing and Alan Roper, *The Works of John Dryden*, Vol. 14: *Plays; The Kind Keeper; The Spanish Fryar; The Duke of Guise; and The Vindication of the Duke of Guise* (Berkley, CA: University of California Press, 1992), 182.

33. Keats, "Ode to Psyche," *Complete Poems*, 341; "Ode on a Grecian Urn," 345; "Ode to a Nightingale," 346.

34. Keats, *Endymion*, Book I, ll. 6–13, *Complete Poems*, 107.

### Lecture III

1. e. e. cummings, *No Thanks*, ed. George Firmage (New York: Liveright, 1978 [1935]), 13. The poem likely dates to around 1932, when cummings

# NOTES

experimented with other shape poems of this kind. See Michael Webster, "Plotting the Evolution of a r-p-o-p-h-e-s-s-a-g-r," *Spring: The Journal of the E. E. Cummings Society*, New series 20 (October 2013): 116–43.

2. William Carlos Williams, "Poem," *The Collected Poems of William Carlos Williams, Volume 1: 1909–1939*, eds. A. Walton Litz and Christopher MacGowan (New York: New Directions, 1991), 352. First published in *Poetry* (July 1930): 195.

3. William Wordsworth, *The Major Works*, ed. Stephen Gill (Oxford: Oxford University Press, 2000), 147. The poem was written in late 1798–early 1799 and first published in Volume II of the 1800 *Lyrical Ballads*.

4. John Beer, "Coleridge, the Wordsworths, and the State of Trance," *The Wordsworth Circle* 8, no. 2 (1977): 121–38.

5. From Richard Crashaw, "Bulla," trans. George Walton Williams, *Complete Poetry of Richard Crashaw* (Garden City, NY: Anchor Books, Doubleday, 1970), 612–20. First published in Daniel Heynsius's *Crepundia Siliana*, 1646, to fill up a blank final page.

6. Percy Shelley, "Hellas," ll. 197–200, written October 1821, published February 1822. *Shelley's Poetry and Prose*, ed. Donald Reiman (New York: Norton, 1977), 416.

7. Carlo Severi, *Capturing Imagination: A Proposal for an Anthropology of Thought*, trans. Catherine V. Howard, Matthew Carey, Eric Bye, Ramon Fonkoue, and Joyce Suechun Cheng (Chicago, IL: Hau Books, University of Chicago Press, 2018), 234–6.

8. Letter to Francis Wrangham, January 18, 1816. *The Letters of William and Dorothy Wordsworth, Vol. 3: The Middle Years: Part II: 1812–1820*, 2nd rev. ed., eds. Ernest De Selincourt, Mary Moorman, and Alan G. Hill (Oxford: Oxford University Press, 1969), 276.

9. John Ruskin, "Of the Pathetic Fallacy," in *Modern Painters*, Volume III, Part IV (New York: John Wiley, 1872), 163.

10. T. S. Eliot, "Hamlet and His Problems," in *The Sacred Wood* (New York: Alfred A. Knopf, 1921), 92.

11. Judith Beck and Lars Konieczny, "Rhythmic subvocalization: An eye-tracking study on silent poetry reading," *Journal of Eye Movement Research* 13, no. 3 (2020), https://doi.org/10.16910/jemr.13.3.5.

12. For renderings of Heraclitus's famous saying "It is not possible to step twice into the same river," see fragments 61, 62, and 63 in *A Presocratics*

## NOTES

*Reader*, ed. Patricia Curd, trans. Richard D. McKirahan (Indianapolis, IN: Hackett, 1995), 36.

13. This definition of a waterfall has been adapted from the Wikipedia entry, "Waterfall": https://en.wikipedia.org/wiki/Waterfall. See the discussion of waterfalls and theories about them by Michael A. Summerfield in his *Global Geomorphology* (London: Routledge, 1991), 219, where he writes: "Given their importance in deciphering the history of river systems, waterfalls have been remarkably little studied. It is widely considered that the great majority of waterfalls develop as a result of the erosion of weak rock from beneath a resistant caprock ..." Summerfield goes on to argue that "the impact of water is probably the predominant mechanism of fluvial erosion operating on waterfalls."

14. Michel Serres, *The Birth of Physics*, trans. David Webb and William Ross (London: Rowan and Littlefield, 2018), 183. Serres is taking a stance against the linguist Émile Benveniste, who had argued against a naturalistic origin for the aesthetics of rhythm and who, to the former sailor Serres's consternation, had thought of fresh water as an undifferentiated, irreversible flow alone. Benveniste, "The Notion of 'Rhythm' in its Linguistic Expression," in *Problems in General Linguistics*, trans. Mary Elizabeth Meek (Miami, FL: University of Miami Press, 1971), 281–8. See the helpful discussion of the history of conflicting theories of rhythm in Vincent Barletta, *Rhythm: Form and Dispossession* (Chicago, IL: University of Chicago Press, 2020). In their essay, "The Water Falls but the Waterfall Does not Fall: New Perspectives on Objects, Processes and Events," Antony Galton and Riichiro Mizoguchi discuss the phenomenon of the waterfall in relation to two binary views on ontology: the "object-priority" argument and the "process-priority" argument. They propose a dynamic "mutual interdependence" between matter, objects, events, and processes as an alternative to this binary. Although their typology itself ends up seeming rather static, their comments on the waterfall as process and object are resonant: "What does the waterfall do? How we answer this depends on exactly what we take the waterfall to be. In fact the most immediately obvious choices for what the waterfall is and what it does are mutually inconsistent: we mean here on the one hand the view of the waterfall as a particular persistent configuration of falling water; and on the other hand, the view that

# NOTES

what a waterfall does is to transfer water from a higher elevation to a lower. The problem with this is that in modelling a waterfall as a device for transferring water, as suggested by the latter view, we are treating a waterfall as a kind of conduit: but a conduit does not include what it conducts as a constituent ... The conduit view of a waterfall is indeed possible, but what it refers to is not the falling water itself (that is, what we normally mean by the waterfall), but rather the interruption to the continuity of the river bed resulting from the presence of the rocky precipice. This is what effects the transfer of water from higher to lower elevation by maintaining a spatial configuration and solidity which allows the water to fall." They point out that as a rocky precipice a waterfall facilitates the transfer of water from a higher to a lower level, and at the same time as a persistent configuration of tumbling water, the waterfall as well is pushing that same rocky precipice upstream. Galton and Mizoguchi, "The Water Falls but the Waterfall Does not Fall: New Perspectives on Objects, Processes and Events," *Applied Ontology* 4, no. 2 (2009): 89–90.

15. Jay Wright, *Soul and Substance, A Poet's Examination Papers* (Princeton, NJ: Princeton University Press, 2023), 411.

16. All quotations from Vaughan's poems are from *Henry Vaughan: The Complete Poems*, ed. Alan Rudrum (New Haven, CT: Yale University Press, 1981). "The Water-fall," 306–7.

17. Demetris Koutsoyiannis and Nikos Mamassis, "From mythology to science: the development of scientific hydrological concepts in Greek antiquity and its relevance to modern hydrology," *Hydrology and Earth System Sciences* 25, no. 5 (2021): 2419–44, https://doi.org/10.5194/hess-25-2419-2021. For the merging of science and theology around concepts in hydrology, see Yi-fu Tuan, *The Hydrological Cycle and the Wisdom of God: A Theme in Geoteleology* (Toronto: University of Toronto Press, 1968).

18. Frank Livingston Huntley, *Bishop Joseph Hall and Protestant Meditation in Seventeenth-Century England: A Study, With the Texts of* The Arte of Divine Meditation (1606) *and* Occasional Meditations (1633) (Binghamton, NY: Center for Medieval and Early Renaissance Studies, 1981). See the discussion of Bishop Hall's text in Donald R. Dickson, "Vaughan's 'The Water-fall' and Protestant Meditation," *Explorations in Renaissance Culture* 10, no. 1 (1984): 28–40.

# NOTES

19. Ted-Larry Pebworth, "The Problem of *Restagnates* in Henry Vaughan's 'The Water-fall'," *Papers on Language and Literature* 3, no. 3 (Summer 1967): 258–9.

20. For Vaughan's turn to "natural religion," see Richard K. Barksdale, "The Nature Poetry of Henry Vaughan," *Western Humanities Review* 9, no. 1 (1955): 341–8.

21. Vaughan, *The Complete Poems*, 219.

22. Aristotle, *Physics*, Book III, Chapter 1: 12: "Nature has been defined as 'a principle of motion and change', and it is the subject of our inquiry. We must therefore see that we understand the meaning of 'motion'; for if it were unknown, the meaning of 'nature' too would be unknown." In *The Basic Works of Aristotle*, ed. Richard McKeon (New York: Random House, 1941), 253.

23. Carl Hoefer, Nick Huggett, and James Read, "Absolute and Relational Space and Motion: Classical Theories," *Stanford Encyclopedia of Philosophy* (Spring 2023 ed.), eds. Edward N. Zalta and Uri Nodelman, https://plato.stanford.edu/archives/spr2023/entries/spacetime-theories-classical/.

24. For questions of Thomas's intellectual influence upon Henry, see Wilson O. Clough, "Henry Vaughan and the Hermetic Philosophy," *PMLA* 48, no. 4 (December 1933): 1108–30, and Ralph M. Wardle, "Thomas Vaughan's Influence upon the Poetry of Henry Vaughan," *PMLA* 51, no. 4 (December 1936): 936–52.

25. Hoefer, Huggett, and Read, "Absolute and Relational."

26. Alfred North Whitehead, *Modes of Thought* (New York: Free Press, Macmillan, 1938), 164–7.

27. Susanne K. Langer, *Mind: An Essay on Human Feeling*, 3 volumes, Volume II (Baltimore, MD and London: The Johns Hopkins University Press, 1972), 215–356 esp.

28. Hans Jonas, *The Phenomenon of Life* (New York: Harper and Row, 1966), 36.

29. For further context to the poem, see the headnote to Percy Shelley, "Mont Blanc," in eds. Donald Reiman and Neil Fraistat, *Shelley's Poetry and Prose* (New York: Norton, 2002), 96; text 97–101, as well as Richard Holmes, *Shelley: The Pursuit* (New York: New York Review Books, 1974), 319–46. For Shelley's comment on never imagining mountains before and sense of wonder, see Mary Shelley and Percy Bysshe Shelley, *History*

# NOTES

*of a Six Weeks' Tour Through a Part of France, Switzerland, Germany, and Holland: With Letters Descriptive of a Sail Around the Lake of Geneva, and the Glaciers of Chamouni* (London: T. Hookham, 1817), letter to Thomas Love Peacock, 151–2.

30. Letters to Elizabeth Hitchener, July 1811 ("Why do they enchant"), p. 119 and October 1811 ("It does not prove the non-existence of a thing"), p. 163. In *Letters of Percy Bysshe Shelley*, Vol. I, ed. Frederick Jones (Oxford: Oxford University Press).

31. The text of the poem is taken from *Gerard Manley Hopkins*, ed. Catherine Phillips (Oxford: Oxford University Press, 1986), 153. The quotation from the letter to Baillie can be found in the notes, p. 366.

32. Phillips notes, p. 366.

33. Phillips notes, pp. 366–8.

34. *The Journals and Papers of Gerard Manley Hopkins*, ed. Humphry House (London: Oxford University Press, 1959), 8.

35. Hopkins, *Journals*, 211.

36. *Gerard Manley Hopkins*, 157–8.

37. From a letter to Robert Bridges, February 26, 1879. *Letters of Gerard Manley Hopkins to Robert Bridges*, ed. Claude Colleer Abbott (Oxford: Oxford University Press, Vol. I), 73–4.

38. *Gerard Manley Hopkins*, 140.

## Lecture IV

1. Emily Dickinson, "A light exists in Spring," *The Poems of Emily Dickinson: Variorum Edition*, 3 vols., ed. Ralph Franklin (Cambridge, MA: Belknap Press of Harvard University Press, 1998). Franklin #962B, 2: 876–7.

2. Hans Jonas, *The Phenomenon of Life* (New York: Harper and Row, 1966), 36.

3. Dickinson, "Faith is a fine invention," *The Poems of Emily Dickinson*, Franklin #202C, 1: 234.

4. From Robert Burns's commonplace book, *Memoranda*, c. 1784, later appended as a preface to reprintings of his 1781 poem, "Winter: A Dirge." In *The Poetical Works of Robert Burns*, ed. Harris Nicolas, 3 vols. (London: W. Pickering, 1839), 1: 146.

## NOTES

5. I take this transcription of the manuscript in British Museum Royal App. 58, fol. 5, from Charles Frey's "Interpreting 'Western Wind,'" *English Literary History* 43, no. 3 (Autumn 1976): 259–78. Frey surveys the many interpretations of the poem and explains the text could have been written by a Tudor courtier, or may perhaps be influenced by oral tradition or a number of medieval English poems characterized by apostrophes to the wind and expressions of erotic longing.

6. *Minor Poems of Michael Drayton*, ed. Cyril Brett (Oxford: Clarendon Press, 1907), 73.

7. Anne Finch [Anne Kingsmill Finch, Countess of Winchilsea], "A Pindarick Poem Upon the Hurricane in November 1703, referring to this Text in Psalm 148. ver. 8. Winds and Storms fulfilling his Word. With a HYMN compos'd of the 148th PSALM Paraphras'd," in *Miscellany Poems, on Several Occasions* (London: printed for J[ohn] B[arber] and sold by Benj. Tooke at the Middle-Temple-Gate, William Taylor in Pater-Noster-Row, and James Round, in Exchange-Alley, Cornhil, 1713), 230–52.

8. Finch, *Miscellany Poems*, 92.

9. Theodore Roethke, "The Storm (*Forio d'Ischia*)," in *The Collected Poems of Theodore Roethke* (New York: Doubleday, 1961), 230–2.

10. The origin of this remark seems to be Jean-Paul Sartre's conversation with Merleau-Ponty as recollected in his memorial essay, "Merleau-Ponty vivant," reprinted in Jon Stewart, ed., *The Debate Between Sartre and Merleau-Ponty* (Evanston, IL: Northwestern University Press, 1998), 614.

11. *The Later Poems of John Clare*, eds. Eric Robinson and David Powell, vol. 2 (Oxford: Clarendon Press, 1984), 611–12.

12. Naomi Schor, *Reading in Detail: Aesthetics and the Feminine* (London: Routledge, 1987). Svetlana Alpers, *The Art of Describing: Dutch Art in the Seventeenth Century* (Chicago, IL: University of Chicago Press, 1984).

13. The letter, dating to April of 1783, is mentioned in Hans Blumenberg, *Work on Myth*, trans. Robert Wallace (Cambridge, MA: MIT Press, 1985), 543, within a longer discussion of Goethe's engagement with the secular implications of Spinoza's ethics.

14. For one of Emerson's more abstract, near-bombastic, nature poems, see Ralph Waldo Emerson, "Song of Nature," in *Collected Poems and Translations*, eds. Harold Bloom and Paul Kane (New York: Library of America,

# NOTES

1994), 186–8. His thoughts on the relations between nature and mind can be found throughout his writings gathered under the heading "Nature; Addresses, and Lectures," in *Essays and Lectures*, ed. Joel Porte (New York: Library of America, 1983), 5–50, and in his argument that poets "participate the invention of nature," in "The Poet," in the same volume, p. 459.

15. On August 13, 1836, Emerson wrote: "Goethe the observer. What sagacity! What industry of observation!" yet is "provoked with his [Goethe's] Olympian self-complacency" and finds Goethe indiscriminate in his interest in all phenomena. On March 21, 1836 he had written that he was drawn to a particularly Spinozan aspect of Goethe's thought: "Only last evening I found the following sentence in Goethe, a comment and consent to my speculations on the All in Each in Nature this last week. 'Every existing thing is an analogon of all existing things. Thence appears to us Being ever, at once sundered & connected. If we follow the analogy too far all things confound themselves in identity. If we avoid it, then all things scatter into infinity. In both cases, observation is at a stand, in the one as too lively, in the other as dead.'" Ralph Waldo Emerson, *Selected Journals, 1820–1842*, ed. Lawrence Rosenwald (New York: Library of America, 2010), 444–8. Goethe is also Emerson's choice of subject for the final entry in his collection of biographies, *Representative Men*. Whereas Shakespeare is designated "The Poet," Goethe's epithet is "The Writer." Emerson's admiration in this work, too, is tempered by his sense of Goethe's "Napoleonic" polymathic ambition. "Goethe; Or, the Writer," in *Essays and Lectures*, ed. Porte, 746–61.

16. Ralph Waldo Emerson, "The Snow-Storm," in *Collected Poems*, eds. Bloom and Kane, 34.

17. Among the prose fragments in Dickinson's papers is "#116," a sheet of paper where she copied Emerson's single line: "Tumultuous privacy of storm." Thomas Johnson writes, "This phrase from Emerson's poem 'The Snow-Storm' ED liked so well, as Mrs. Bingham points out, that she copied it onto a sheet of stationery, put it in quotes, and enclosed it in a letter which Lavinia wrote to Mrs. Todd, 5 February 1884." *The Letters of Emily Dickinson*, 3 vols., eds. Thomas H. Johnson and Theodora Ward (Cambridge, MA: Harvard University Press, 1958), 3: 928.

## NOTES

18. Henry David Thoreau, "Walking," *The Atlantic* 9, no. 56 (June 1862): 657–74.

19. Texts are from *Whitman: Complete Poetry and Collected Prose*, ed. Justin Kaplan (New York: Library of America, 1982): "On the Beach at Night," 398–9; "The World Below the Brine," 399–400; "On the Beach at Night Alone," 400–1.

20. "Sunday Evening Lectures" discussion of Kant, Hegel, Schelling, and Fichte. I have consulted the controversial 1902 edition by Richard Maurice Bucke available in *Notebooks and Unpublished Prose Manuscripts: Walt Whitman*, 6 vols., ed. Edward F. Grier (New York: New York University Press, 1984), 6: 2009–18, but the order of these comments on German metaphysics, the manuscript of which is now held in the Harry Ransom Center at the University of Texas, remains unresolved. For recent attempts at creating facsimiles and an order for Whitman's unnumbered pages, see Gary Wihl, "The Manuscript of Walt Whitman's 'Sunday Evening Lectures'," *Walt Whitman Quarterly Review* 18, no. 3 (Winter 2001), 107–33. The Fichte discussion can be found on pp. 122–3. For our purposes, Whitman's attraction to Fichte's ideas about the relation between point of view and the perception of nature and the "essential identity of subjective and objective worlds" is most relevant.

21. Marianne Moore, *Complete Poems of Marianne Moore* (New York: Penguin, 1981), 49–50.

22. Marianne Moore, *The Complete Prose of Marianne Moore*, ed. Patricia C. Willis (New York: Penguin, 1987), 643. Moore's comments on the origin of the poem originally appeared in *Fifty Poets*, ed. William Rose Benét (New York: Duffield and Green, 1933), 84–5.

23. Letter to Ezra Pound, January 9, 1919, reprinted as "A Letter to Ezra Pound," in *Marianne Moore, A Collection of Critical Essays*, ed. Charles Tomlinson (Englewood Cliffs, NJ: Prentice Hall, 1969), 17.

24. M. H. Abrams, "Structure and Style in the Greater Romantic Lyric," in *The Correspondent Breeze: Essays on English Romanticism* (New York: W. W. Norton, 1984), 76–108.

25. Friedrich Nietzsche, *Beyond Good and Evil*, in *Basic Writings of Nietzsche*, trans. and ed. Walter Kaufmann (New York: Modern Library, 1968), 181–438, 205.

# WORKS CITED

Abrahams, Roger D. and George Foss. *Anglo-American Folksong Style*. Englewood Cliffs, NJ: Prentice-Hall, 1968.

Abrams, M. H. "Structure and Style in the Greater Romantic Lyric." In *The Correspondent Breeze: Essays on English Romanticism*, 76–108. New York: W. W. Norton, 1984.

Alpers, Svetlana. *The Art of Describing: Dutch Art in the Seventeenth Century*. Chicago, IL: University of Chicago Press, 1984.

Aquinas, Thomas. *De Divinis Nominibus*. https://documentacatholicaomnia.eu/03d/1225-1274,_Thomas_Aquinas,_In_Dionysii_de_Divinis_Nominibus,_LT.pdf

Aquinas, Thomas. *Summa Theologica. New English Translation of St. Thomas Aquinas's Summa Theologiae (Summa Theologica)* by Alfred J. Freddoso, University of Notre Dame. https://www3.nd.edu/~afreddos/summa-translation/TOC-part1-2.htm

Aristotle, *Poetics*. Translated by Richard Janko. Indianapolis, IN: Hackett, 1987.

Aristotle. *Nicomachean Ethics*. Translated by Terence Irwin, 2nd ed. Indianapolis, IN and Cambridge, MA: Hackett, 1999.

Aristotle. *Physics*. In *The Basic Works of Aristotle*. Edited by Richard McKeon and translated by R. P. Hardie and R. K. Gaye, 213–394. New York: Random House, 1941.

Auden, W. H. *The Poet's Tongue*. Edited by W. H. Auden and John Garrett. London: G. Bell & Sons, 1935.

Augustine, *Confessions*. Translated by R. S. Pine-Coffin. London: Penguin, 1962.

Barksdale, Richard K. "The Nature Poetry of Henry Vaughan." *Western Humanities Review* 9, no. 1 (1955): 341–8.

Barletta, Vincent. *Rhythm: Form and Dispossession*. Chicago, IL: University of Chicago Press, 2020.

# WORKS CITED

Beck, Judith and Lars Konieczny. "Rhythmic subvocalization: An eye-tracking study on silent poetry reading." *Journal of Eye Movement Research* 13, no. 3 (2020). https://doi.org/10.16910/jemr.13.3.5

Beer, John. "Coleridge, the Wordsworths, and the State of Trance." *The Wordsworth Circle* 8, no. 2 (1977): 121–38.

Benét, William Rose, ed. *Fifty Poets*. New York: Duffield and Green, 1933.

Benveniste, Émile. "The Notion of 'Rhythm' in its Linguistic Expression." In *Problems in General Linguistics*. Translated by Mary Elizabeth Meek, 281–8. Miami, FL: University of Miami Press, 1971.

Blumenberg, Hans. *Work on Myth*. Translated by Robert Wallace. Cambridge, MA: MIT Press, 1985.

Bodleian Douce 139 f 5.r. *Bodleian Summary Catalogue* Vol. IV, 534–5.

Bronson, Bertrand Harris. *The Traditional Tunes of the Child Ballads*, vol. 1. Princeton, NJ: Princeton University Press, 1959.

Brown, Carleton. *English Lyrics of the XIIIth Century*. Oxford: Oxford University Press, 1932.

Burns, Robert. *The Poetical Works of Robert Burns*, vol. 1. Edited by Harris Nicolas. London: W. Pickering, 1839.

Child, James, ed. *The English and Scottish Popular Ballads*, vol. 5. New York: Dover, 1965.

Clare, John. *The Later Poems of John Clare*, vol. 2. Edited by Eric Robinson and David Powell. Oxford: Clarendon Press, 1984.

Clare, John. "The Progress of Rhyme." 1824–43. In *The Midsummer Cushion*, edited by R. K. R. Thornton and Anne Tibble, 224–32. Manchester: Mid-Northumberland Arts Group, Carcanet Press, 1990.

Clough, Wilson O. "Henry Vaughan and the Hermetic Philosophy." *PMLA* 48, no. 4 (December 1933): 1108–30.

Collingwood, R. G. *The Idea of Nature*. New York: Oxford University Press, Galaxy Books, 1960.

Conway Morris, Simon. *Life's Solution: Inevitable Humans in a Lonely Universe*. Cambridge: Cambridge University Press, 2003.

Cowper, William. "'Review' of Erasmus Darwin's *Economy of Vegetation*." In *The Analytical Review or History of Literature, Domestic and Foreign, on an Enlarged Plan*, vol. XV (January–May 1793), 287–93. London: J. Johnson, 1793.

Cowper, William. *Correspondence of William Cowper, Arranged in Chronological Order*, vol. 3. Edited by Thomas Wright. London: Hodder & Stoughton, 1904.

# WORKS CITED

Cox, Jeffrey N., ed. *Keats's Poetry and Prose*. New York: Norton, 2009.

Crashaw, Richard. *Complete Poetry of Richard Crashaw*. Translated by George Walton Williams. Garden City, NY: Anchor Books, Doubleday, 1970.

cummings, e. e. *No Thanks*. Edited by George Firmage. New York: Liveright, 1978 [1935].

Dean, James M. "Mood Imperative: The Cuckoo, the Latin Lyrics, and the 'Cuckoo Song'." *Philological Quarterly* 85, nos. 3, 4 (Summer, Fall 2006): 207–22.

Deleuze, Gilles. *Difference and Repetition*. Translated by Paul Patton. London: Continuum, 2004.

Descola, Philippe. "Constructing natures: symbolic ecology and social practice." In *Nature and Society: Anthropological Perspectives*. Edited by Philippe Descola and Gísli Pálsson, 82–102. London: Routledge, 1996.

Dickinson, Emily. *The Letters of Emily Dickinson*, vol. 3. Edited by Thomas H. Johnson and Theodora Ward. Cambridge, MA: Harvard University Press, 1958.

Dickinson, Emily. *The Poems of Emily Dickinson: Variorum Edition*, vol. 3. Edited by Ralph Franklin. Cambridge, MA: Belknap Press of Harvard University Press, 1998.

Dickson, Donald R. "Vaughan's 'The Water-fall' and Protestant Meditation." *Explorations in Renaissance Culture* 10, no. 1 (1984): 28–40.

Douglas, Gavin. *The Eneados, 1513*. In *Gavin Douglas's Translation of Virgil's Aeneid*, vol. 3. Edited by Priscilla Bawcutt with Ian Cunningham. The Scottish Text Society, Edinburgh, 2020–22.

Drayton, Michael. *Minor Poems of Michael Drayton*. Edited by Cyril Brett. Oxford: Clarendon Press, 1907.

Dryden, John. *The Spanish Fryar*. In *The Works of John Dryden, vol. 14: Plays; The Kind Keeper; The Spanish Fryar; The Duke of Guise; and The Vindication of the Duke of Guise*. Edited by Vinton A. Dearing and Alan Roper. Berkeley, CA: University of California Press, 1992.

Dunbar, William. *The Complete Works*. Edited by John Conlee. Kalamazoo, MI: Medieval Institute Publications, 2004.

Eliot, T. S. "Hamlet and His Problems." In *The Sacred Wood*, 87–94. New York: Alfred A. Knopf, 1921.

Emerson, Ralph Waldo. *Essays and Lectures*. Edited by Joel Porte. *New York: Library of America*, 1983.

Emerson, Ralph Waldo. *Collected Poems and Translations*. Edited by Harold Bloom and Paul Lane. New York: Library of America, 1994.

# WORKS CITED

Emerson, Ralph Waldo. *Selected Journals, 1820–1842*. Edited by Lawrence Rosenwald. New York: Library of America, 2010.

Fairer, David and Christine Gerrard, eds. *Eighteenth-Century Poetry: An Annotated Anthology*. Chichester: John Wiley, 2015.

Finch, Anne [Anne Kingsmill Finch, *Countess of Winchilsea*]. *Miscellany Poems, on Several Occasions*. London: printed for J[ohn] B[arber] and sold by Benj. Tooke at the Middle-Temple-Gate, William Taylor in Pater-Noster-Row, and James Round, in Exchange-Alley, Cornhil, 1713.

Fischer, Luke and David Macauley, eds. *The Seasons: Philosophical, Literary, and Environmental Perspectives*. Albany, NY: SUNY Press, 2021.

French, Roger. "Aristotle and the Nature of Things." In *Ancient Natural History*, 5–67. London: Routledge, 1994.

Frey, Charles. "Interpreting 'Western Wind'." *English Literary History* 43, no. 3 (Autumn 1976): 259–78.

Frye, Northrop. *Anatomy of Criticism*. Princeton, NJ: Princeton University Press, 1957.

Galton, Anthony and Mizoguchi, Riichiro. "The Water Falls but the Waterfall Does not Fall: New Perspectives on Objects, Processes and Events." *Applied Ontology* 4, no. 2 (2009): 71–107.

Godfrey-Smith, Peter. *Metazoa: Animal Life and the Birth of the Mind*. New York: Farrar Straus, 2020.

Gorji, Mina. *John Clare and the Place of Poetry*. Liverpool: Liverpool University Press, 2008.

Hadot, Pierre. *The Veil of Isis: An Essay on the History of the Idea of Nature*. Translated by Michael Chase. Boston, MA: Harvard University Press, 2006.

Hauser, Marc and Peter Marler. *Phonological Development: Models, Research, Implications*. Edited by C. A. Ferguson et al. Timonium, MD: York Press, 1992.

Hawes, Bess Lomax. "Folksongs and Function: Some Thoughts on the American Lullaby." *Journal of American Folklore* 87, no. 344 (April–June 1974): 140–8.

Hayley, William. *Supplementary pages to the Life of Cowper: containing the additions made to that work on reprinting it in octavo*. Chichester: J. Seagrave for J. Johnson, 1806.

Helsinger, Elizabeth. "Poem Into Song." *New Literary History* 46, no. 4 (Autumn 2015): 669–90.

Heraclitus. *A Presocratics Reader*. Edited by Patricia Curd, translated by Richard D. McKirahan. Indianapolis, IN: Hackett, 1995.

## WORKS CITED

Higginson, William J. *Haiku Seasons: Poetry of the Natural World.* Berkeley, CA: Stone Bridge Press, 2008.

Hoefer, Carl, Nick Huggett, and James Read. "Absolute and Relational Space and Motion: Classical Theories." *Stanford Encyclopedia of Philosophy* (Spring 2023 ed.). Edited by Edward N. Zalta and Uri Nodelman. https:// plato.stanford.edu/archives/spr2023/entries/spacetime-theories-classical/

Holmes, Richard. *Shelley: The Pursuit.* New York: New York Review Books, 1974.

Hopkins, Gerard Manley. *Letters of Gerard Manley Hopkins to Robert Bridges.* Edited by Claude Colleer Abbott. Oxford: Oxford University Press, 1955.

Hopkins, Gerard Manley. *The Journals and Papers of Gerard Manley Hopkins.* Edited by Humphry House. London: Oxford University Press, 1959.

Hopkins, Gerard Manley. *Gerard Manley Hopkins.* Edited by Catherine Phillips. Oxford: Oxford University Press, 1986.

Huntley, Frank Livingston. *Bishop Joseph Hall and Protestant Meditation in Seventeenth-Century England: A Study, With the Texts of The Arte of Divine Meditation (1606) and Occasional Meditations (1633).* Binghamton, NY: Center for Medieval and Early Renaissance Studies, 1981.

Jarvis, Erich D. "Evolution of Brain Pathways for Vocal Learning in Birds and Humans." In *Birdsong, Speech, and Language: Exploring the Evolution of Mind and Brain.* Edited by Johan J. Bolhuis and Martin Everaert, 63–107. Cambridge, MA: MIT Press, 2013.

Jarvis, Erich D. *Jarvis Lab.* Rockefeller University. www.jarvislab.net

Jensen, Richard d'A. "Birdsong and the Imitation of Birdsong in the Music of the Middle Ages and the Renaissance." *Current Musicology* 40, no. 1 (January 1985): 50–65.

Jonas, Hans. *The Phenomenon of Life.* New York: Harper and Row, 1966.

Kant, Immanuel. *The Critique of Pure Reason.* Edited and translated by Paul Guyer and Allen Wood. Cambridge: Cambridge University Press, 1998.

Kay, Sarah. *Parrots and Nightingales: Troubadour Quotations and the Development of European Poetry.* Philadelphia, PA: University of Pennsylvania Press, 2013.

Keats, John. *The Complete Poems.* Edited by John Barnard. 3rd ed. London: Penguin Books, 1988.

Kehew, Robert, ed. *Lark in the Morning: The Verses of the Troubadours.* Translated by Ezra Pound, W. D. Snodgrass, and Robert Kehew. Chicago, IL: University of Chicago Press, 2005.

## WORKS CITED

King, James. *William Cowper: A Biography.* Durham, NC: Duke University Press, 1986.

Koutsoyiannis, Demetris and Nikos Mamassis. "From mythology to science: the development of scientific hydrological concepts in Greek antiquity and its relevance to modern hydrology." *Hydrology and Earth System Sciences* 25, no. 5 (2021): 2419–44. https://doi.org/10.5194/hess-25-2419-2021

Langer, Susanne K. *Mind: An Essay on Human Feeling*, vol. 2. Baltimore, MD and London: The Johns Hopkins University Press, 1972.

Lord, Albert. *The Singer of Tales*, 3rd ed. *Milman Parry Collection of Oral Literature.* Cambridge, MA: Harvard University Press, 2019.

Lovejoy, Arthur O. "'Nature' as Aesthetic Norm." In *Essays in the History of Ideas*, 69–77. Baltimore, MD: The Johns Hopkins University Press, 1948.

Lovejoy, Arthur O. and George Boas. "Some Meanings of 'Nature'," *Appendix.* In *Primitivism and Related Ideas in Antiquity*, 447–56. Baltimore, MD: The Johns Hopkins University Press, 1935.

Lucash, Frank. "Spinoza's Two Views of Substance." *Dialogue: Revue canadienne de philosophie* 50, no. 3 (September 2011): 537–55.

Macauley, David. "The Four Seasons and the Rhythms of Place-Based Time." In *The Seasons: Philosophical, Literary, and Environmental Perspectives.* Edited by Luke Fischer and David Macauley, 27–52. Albany, NY: SUNY Press, 2021.

Margulis, Lynn and Dorion Sagan, *What Is Life?* Berkeley, CA: University of California Press, 1995.

Mauss, Marcel, in collaboration with Henri Beuchat. *Seasonal Variations of the Eskimo: A Study in Social Morphology.* Translated by James J. Fox. London: Routledge & Kegan Paul, 1979.

Meyer, Steven. Introduction to "Whitehead Now." *Configurations* 13, no. 1 (Winter 2005): 1–33.

Moore, Marianne. Letter to Ezra Pound, January 9, 1919. In *Marianne Moore, A Collection of Critical Essays.* Edited by Charles Tomlinson, 16–18. Englewood Cliffs, NJ: Prentice Hall, 1969.

Moore, Marianne. *Complete Poems of Marianne Moore.* New York: Penguin, 1981.

Moore, Marianne. *The Complete Prose of Marianne Moore.* Edited by Patricia C. Willis. New York: Penguin, 1987.

Moser, Thomas C. "'And I Mon Waxe Wod': The Middle English 'Foweles in the Frith'." *PMLA* 102, no. 3 (May 1987): 326–37.

## WORKS CITED

Nardizzi, Vin. "Shakespeare's Penknife: Grafting and Seedless Generation in the Procreation Sonnets." *Renaissance and Reformation* 32, no. 1 (Winter 2009): 83–106.

Nietzsche, Friedrich. *Beyond Good and Evil*. In *Basic Writings of Nietzsche*. Edited and translated by Walter Kaufmann, 181–438. New York: Modern Library, 1968.

Nurse, Paul. *What Is Life?: Five Great Ideas in Biology*. New York: Norton, 2020.

Parkinson, R. B. *Voices from Ancient Egypt: An Anthology of Middle Kingdom Writings*. London: British Museum Press, 1991.

Pebworth, Ted-Larry. "The Problem of *Restagnates* in Henry Vaughan's 'The Water-fall'." *Papers on Language and Literature* 3, no. 3 (Summer 1967): 258–9.

Petrarch, Francesco. *Petrarch's Lyric Poems: The Rime Sparse and Other Lyrics*. Edited and translated by Robert Durling. Cambridge, MA: Harvard University Press, 1976.

Plato. *Plato's Cosmology: The Timaeus of Plato*. Translated by Francis M. Cornford. London: Routledge, 1937.

Plato. *Sophist*. Translated by Seth Bernadete. Chicago, IL: University of Chicago Press, 1984.

Pound, Ezra. *Instigations*. New York: Boni and Liveright, 1920.

Pound, Ezra. *ABC of Reading*. London: Faber, 1951.

Pound, Ezra. *The Spirit of Romance*. New York: New Directions, 1968.

Resvick, Jessica. "Wechsel-Dauer (Change-Constancy)." *Goethe-Lexicon of Philosophical Concepts* 3 (December 2022). https://doi.org/10.5195/glpc.2022.54

Ringler, Richard N. "The Genesis of Cowper's 'Yardley Oak'." *English Language Notes* 5, no. 1 (1967): 27–32.

Roethke, Theodore. *Collected Poems of Theodore Roethke*. New York: Doubleday, 1961.

Roscow, G. H. "What is 'Sumer Is Icumen In'?" *The Review of English Studies* 50, no. 198 (May 1999): 188–95.

Rovelli, Carlo. *Reality Is Not What It Seems: The Journey to Quantum Gravity*. Translated by Simon Carnell and Erica Segre. New York: Riverhead Books, 2017.

Rowlinson, Matthew. "Onomatopoeia, Interiority, and Incorporation." *Studies in Romanticism* 57, no. 3 (Fall 2018): 429–51.

Ruskin, John. "Of the Pathetic Fallacy." In *Modern Painters*, vol. 3, Part IV, 156–72. New York: John Wiley, 1872.

## WORKS CITED

Ryskamp, Charles. "Cowper and Darwin's *Economy of Vegetation*." *Harvard Library Bulletin* 9, no. 3 (Autumn 1957): 317–18.

Sartre, Jean-Paul. "Merleau-Ponty vivant." Reprinted in *The Debate Between Sartre and Merleau-Ponty*. Edited by Jon Stewart, 565–626. Evanston, IL: Northwestern University Press, 1998.

Schor, Naomi. *Reading in Detail: Aesthetics and the Feminine*. London: Routledge, 1987.

Serres, Michel. *The Birth of Physics*. Translated by David Webb and William Ross. London: Rowan and Littlefield, 2018.

Severi, Carlo. *Capturing Imagination: A Proposal for an Anthropology of Thought*. Translated by Catherine V. Howard, Matthew Carey, Eric Bye, Ramon Fonkoue, and Joyce Suechun Cheng. Chicago, IL: Hau Books, University of Chicago Press, 2018.

Shelley, Mary and Percy Bysshe Shelley. *History of a Six Weeks' Tour Through a Part of France, Switzerland, Germany, and Holland: With Letters Descriptive of a Sail Around the Lake of Geneva, and the Glaciers of Chamouni*. London: T. Hookham, 1817.

Shelley, Percy Bysshe. *Letters of Percy Bysshe Shelley*. Edited by Frederick Jones. Oxford: Oxford University Press, 1964.

Shelley, Percy Bysshe. *Shelley's Poetry and Prose*. Edited by Donald Reiman. New York: Norton, 1977.

Shelley, Percy Bysshe. *Shelley's Poetry and Prose*. Edited by Donald Reiman and Neil Fraistat. New York: Norton, 2002.

Sidney, Sir Philip. *Selected Poems*. Edited by Catherine Bates. London: Penguin, 1994.

Spenser, Edmund. *The Shorter Poems*. Edited by Richard McCabe. London: Penguin, 1999.

Spinoza, Benedict de. *Ethics. In On the Improvement of the Understanding, the Ethics, Correspondence*. Translated by R. H. M. Elwes, 42–272. New York: Dover, 1955.

Stark, Robert. *Ezra Pound's Early Verse and Lyric Tradition: A Jargoner's Apprenticeship*. Edinburgh: Edinburgh University Press, 2012.

Stengers, Isabelle. *Thinking with Whitehead: A Free and Wild Creation of Concepts*. Translated by Michael Chase. Cambridge, MA: Harvard University Press, 2014.

Stevens, Wallace. *Letters of Wallace Stevens*. Edited by Holly Stevens. New York: Knopf, 1966.

# WORKS CITED

Stevens, Wallace. *Stevens: Collected Poetry and Prose*. Edited by Frank Kermode and Joan Richardson. New York: Library of America, 1997.

Stillinger, Jack. *The Texts of Keats's Poems*. Cambridge, MA: Harvard University Press, 1974.

Su, Hui and Lin Yinbo. "A Comparative Study on the Man–Nature Relationship and Its Presentation in Chinese and British Nature Poetry." *Forum for World Literature Studies* 7, no. 4 (December 2015): 633–42.

"Sumer Is Icumen In." *British Library MS Harley 978*, Folio 11v.

Summerfield, Michael A. *Global Geomorphology*. London: Routledge, 1991.

Thoreau, Henry David. "Walking." *The Atlantic* 9, no. 56 (June 1862): 657–74.

Tuan, Yi-fu. *The Hydrological Cycle and the Wisdom of God: A Theme in Geoteleology*. Toronto: University of Toronto Press, 1968.

Tuve, Rosemond. *Seasons and Months: Studies in a Tradition of Middle English Poetry*. D.S. Brewer, and Totowa, NJ: Rowman and Littlefield, 1933.

Unger, Christoph. "A re-analysis of genre and its implications for pragmatics." In *Genre, Relevance, and Global Coherence: The Pragmatics of Discourse Type*, 253–68. London: Palgrave Macmillan, 2006.

Vaughan, Henry. *Henry Vaughan: The Complete Poems*. Edited by Alan Rudrum. New Haven, CT: Yale University Press, 1981.

Waley, Arthur, trans. *The Book of Songs: The Ancient Chinese Classic of Poetry*. New York: Grove Press, 1996.

Wardle, Ralph M. "Thomas Vaughan's Influence upon the Poetry of Henry Vaughan." *PMLA* 51, no. 4 (December 1936): 936–52.

Webster, Michael. "Plotting the Evolution of a r-p-o-p-h-e-s-s-a-g-r." *Spring: The Journal of the E. E. Cummings Society*, no. 20 (October 2013): 116–43.

"Western Wind." *British Museum Royal App.* 58, fol. 5.

White, Hayden. "The Structure of Historical Narrative." In *The Fiction of Narrative: Essays on History, Literature, and Theory, 1957–2007*. Edited by Robert Doran, 112–25. Baltimore, MD: The Johns Hopkins University Press, 2010.

Whitehead, Alfred North. *Concept of Nature*. Cambridge: Cambridge University Press, 1920.

Whitehead, Alfred North. *Science and the Modern World*. New York: Macmillan, 1925.

Whitehead, Alfred North. *Modes of Thought*. New York: Free Press, Macmillan, 1938.

Whitley, Alvin. "The autograph of Keats's 'In Drear nighted December'." *Harvard Library Bulletin* 5, no. 1 (Winter 1951): 116–22.

## WORKS CITED

Whitman, Walt. *Whitman: Complete Poetry and Collected Prose.* Edited by Justin Kaplan. New York: Library of America, 1982.

Whitman, Walt. "Sunday Evening Lectures." Edited by Richard Maurice Bucke, reprinted in *Notebooks and Unpublished Prose Manuscripts: Walt Whitman,* vol. 6. Edited by Edward F. Grier. New York: New York University Press, 1984.

Wihl, Gary. "The Manuscript of Walt Whitman's 'Sunday Evening Lectures'." *Walt Whitman Quarterly Review* 18, no. 3 (Winter 2001), 107–33.

Wikipedia. "Waterfall." Last modified April 23, 2024. https://en.wikipedia.org/wiki/Waterfall

Williams, Heather. "Birdsong and Singing Behavior." *Annals of the New York Academy of Sciences,* no. 1016 (June 2004): 1–30.

Williams, William Carlos. *The Collected Poems of William Carlos Williams, vol. 1: 1909–1939.* Edited by A. Walton Litz and Christopher MacGowan. New York: New Directions, 1991.

Wilson, E. O. "Bibliophilia." In *E. O. Wilson.* Edited by David Quammen, 5–128. New York: Library of America, 1991.

Wimsatt, W. K. "One Relation of Rhyme to Reason: Alexander Pope." *Modern Language Quarterly* 5, no. 3 (September 1944): 323–38.

Wimsatt, W. K. "Verbal Style: Logical and Counterlogical." *PMLA* 65, no. 2 (March 1950): 5–20.

Wordsworth, William. *The Major Works.* Edited by Stephen Gill. Oxford: Oxford University Press, 2000.

Wordsworth, William and Dorothy Wordsworth. *The Letters of William and Dorothy Wordsworth, vol. 3: The Middle Years: Part II: 1812–1820.* Edited by Ernest De Selincourt, Mary Moorman, and Alan G. Hill. 2nd rev. ed. Oxford: Oxford University Press, 1969.

Wright, Jay. *Soul and Substance, A Poet's Examination Papers.* Princeton, NJ: Princeton University Press, 2023.

Wright, Thomas. *The Life of William Cowper.* New York: Haskell House, 1892.

Wu, Duncan. "'In Drear-Nighted December': The Newly Acquired KSMA Manuscript." *Keats–Shelley Review* 32, no. 1 (2018): 22–7.

# INDEX

*For the benefit of digital users, indexed terms that span two pages (e.g., 52–53) may, on occasion, appear on only one of those pages.*

## A

Abrahams, Roger 20
Abrams, M. H. 107
albas 6–7, 99
Alpers, Svetlana 95
animal calls and behavior 7, 9–12, 57–58
Aquinas, Thomas 3–4
Ariosto, Ludovico 51–52
Aristotle 3, 5, 27–28, 68–69, 71–72, 107
Arnaut Daniel 16–17
  "Can chai la fueilla" 36–37
  "Doutz Brais e Critz" 17
Auden, W. H. 8–9
Augustine, St 32–33

## B

Bailey, Benjamin 49
Baillie, W. M. 78–79
ballads 17–18, 21
Berkeley, George 72
Bernart de Ventadorn
  "Can l'erba 'fresch'" 36–37
Berry, Duc de 34
birdsong 9–10, 12–17
birth 41
Bridges, Robert 82–83
Bruno, Giordano 102–103
Buffon, Georges-Louis Leclerc, Comte de 78
Burns, Robert 88–89

## C

causality 3, 64–65, 72–74
Child ballads 17–18
China, and seasons 6–7
Christianity, and seasons 36
Clare, John
  "Clock a Clay" 28–30, 94
  "Progress of Rhyme, The" 14–15
Coleridge, Samuel Taylor 55, 60
  *Rime of the Ancient Mariner, The* 16
Collingwood, R. G. 31–32
Cowper, William 49
  "Yardley Oak" 43–49
Cowper's Oak 44, 45*f*
Crashaw, Richard
  "Bulla" 61–62
creativity 5–6
cuckoos 10–11
cummings, e. e.
  "r-p-o-p-h-e-s-s-a-g-r" 57–59

## D

Dante 17
Darwin, Erasmus 44–46
death 18, 24, 39–40, 60, 69–70, 75–76, 93–94
Deleuze, Gilles 34
Descartes, René 12, 72
detail 95–96
Dickinson, Emily
  "'Faith' is a fine invention" 86

# INDEX

Dickinson, Emily (*Continued*)
  "light exists in Spring, A" 85–87
Douglas, Gavin 37–38
Drayton, Michael
  "Ode Written in the Peake, An" 90
Dryden, John 51–52
Dunbar, William
  "Meditation In Winter, A" 37–38
duration *see* time

## E

Ecclesiastes 36, 68–69
eclogues 6–7
Egypt, ancient, religious hymns 6–7
Eleusinian mysteries 36
Eliot, T. S. 62–63
Emerson, Ralph Waldo 96–97
  "Snow Storm, The" 96–100
enjambment 42, 59, 63, 80

## F

fertility and growth 10–11, 18, 20–21, 35,
  39–43, 92
Fichte, Johann Gottlieb 104
Finch, Anne
  "Pindaric Poem Upon the Hurricane
    in November 1703, A" 90–92
  "Spleen, The" 91
"Foweles in the frith" 36–37
Frye, Northrop 33

## G

Galileo Galilei 72
georgics 6–7
Goethe, Johann Wolfgang von 35, 96
Greece, ancient
  and nature 2–3
  and seasons 36
growth *see* fertility and growth
Guiraut de Bornelh
  "Can lo freitz e·l glatz e la neus" 36–37

## H

Hadot, Pierre 2–3
*haiga* 36
*haiku* 36
Hall, Joseph 69
Hawes, Bess Lomax 19
Hayley, William 44–46, 45*f*
Heraclitus 64
history and history writing 27–28, 30–32,
  47–48
Homer 12, 48–49
Hopkins, Gerard Manley
  "Inversnaid" 78–83
  "O where is it, the wilderness?" 82–83
  "Trio of Triolets" 82–83
  "Woodlark, The" 13–14
Horace 39–40
Hume, David 73

## I

idylls 6–7
interiority 88–89, 93, 98

## J

Japan, and seasons 36, 39
jargon 16
Jarvis, Erich 13
Johnson, John 44
Jonas, Hans 73–74, 86

## K

Kant, Immanuel 4, 23–24, 73, 96, 108
Keats, John 60
  *Endymion* 50–52, 53–54
  "Human Seasons, The" 49–50
  "In drear-nighted December" 50–54
  "Ode on a Grecian Urn" 52–53
  "Ode to a Nightingale" 52–53
  "Ode to Psyche" 52–53
*kigo* 36

# INDEX

## L

Langer, Susanne 73
Leibniz, Gottfried Wilhelm 72
Leopardi, Giacomo
 "Infinito, L'" 107
Lomax, Alan 19
Lord, Albert 21
lullabies 18–19

## M

Mauss, Marcel 35
meaning 6
medieval poetry 9, 16–17, 35–41, 90
Meen, Margaret 45*f*
Merleau-Ponty, Maurice 94
Moore, Marianne
 "Grave, A" 104–107
More, Henry 72
mortality *see* death
motion 57–59, 62–64, 71–73

## N

narrative 30–33
nature
 and creativity 5–6
 and God 96
 and growth 41–43
 and motion 71–73
 as overwhelming 88–89
 perception of 4–5, 87, 94
 as a totality 5–6
 Western view of 1–6
nature poems 6–7
*natura naturans* and *natura naturata* 3–4,
 24, 96
Newton, Sir Isaac 72
Nietzsche, Friedrich 107
nocturnes 6–7, 99
nonsemantic devices *see under* poetry
nonsense refrains 19, 21
noumenal 4, 6, 21

## O

Oswald, Alice
 *Dart* 64
 "O westward wind" 89

## P

Pack, Robert 22
Palissy, Bernard 68–69
Parry, Milman 21
"Parsley, sage, rosemary, and thyme" 20
pastorals 6–7
personification 62–63
Peter Lombard 71–72
Petrarch
 Rime 9 39–41
Phillips, Catherine 80–82
*physis* 2
Plato 2–3, 68–69
Pliny the Elder 68–69
poems, nature *see* nature poems
poetry
 as counterlogical 8–9
 creation of 6–7, 33
 history writing vs. 27–28, 30–32
 and intelligibility 9, 15–16
 and nonsemantic devices 7–9, 17–18,
  20–21, 27
 and nonsense 17, 19, 21
poetry, medieval *see* medieval poetry
*poiesis* 34
Pound, Ezra 16–17, 21–22, 106
prosopopoeia 62–63

## R

Reading Abbey 9
rhyme 8–9
rhythm 6, 8–9, 66
Roethke, Theodore
 "Storm: *Forio d'Ischia*, The" 92–94
Rovelli, Carlo 5
Ruskin, John 62–63

# INDEX

## S

Schor, Naomi 95
sea and seaside 100–106
seasons 11–12, 28–29, 33, 34–38, 49–50
Seneca 68–69
Serres, Michel 65–66, 82
Severi, Carlo 62–63
Shakespeare, William 10–11
  sonnets 38–39, 41–43
Shelley, Percy Bysshe 5–6, 8–9, 74
  "Hellas" 62
  "Mont Blanc" 74–77, 107
Shi-ching *Book of Songs* 6–7
Sidney, Sir Philip
  "Astrophil and Stella" 41
Skelton, John 68
Spenser, Edmund
  *Amoretti* 41
Spinoza, Baruch 3–4, 96, 107
Stark, Robert 16
Stevens, Wallace
  "Course of a Particular, The" 21–24
storms and wind 88–94, 96–98
sublime, the 6, 88, 107
subvocalization 63
"Sumer is icumen in" 9–11, 35

## T

Thomson, James 11–12
Thoreau, Henry David 100
time 5–6, 27, 28–29, 30–31, 32–33, 44–48, 99
Trager, Edith 19
Très Riches Heures du Duc de Berry 34
Tuve, Rosemond 38–39
"Twa Corbies, The" 18

## V

Vaughan, Henry 72, 74

"Affliction" 70
"The Water-fall" 65, 66–68, 69–71
Vaughan, Thomas 72
Vegius, Maphaeus 37–38
Virgil 12, 37–38
vowel sounds 19, 21

## W

water and waterfalls 64–69, 78–80, 82
Watson, Caroline 45*f*
weather 11–12
White, Hayden 31
Whitehead, Alfred North 4–6, 72–73, 94
Whitman, Walt
  "On the Beach at Night" 100–101,
    102–103
  "On the Beach at Night Alone" 100–101,
    103–104
  "Sea-Drift" 100–101
  "World below the Brine, The" 100–103
wilderness 76–77, 82–83, 87–88
William of Ockham 71–72
Williams, George Walton 61
Williams, Heather 12
Williams, William Carlos 58–59
Wilson, E. O. 12–13
Wimsatt, W. K. 8–9
wind *see* storms and wind
Wordsworth, William 5–6, 62–63
  Intimations Ode 68
  River Duddon sonnets 64
  "slumber did my spirit seal, A" 59–61,
    63–64
Wright, Jay 66
"Wynter wakeneth al my care" 37–38

## Y

Yardley Oak (Cowper's Oak) 44, 45*f*